How to
Lose the
Hounds

How to Lose the Hounds

MAROON GEOGRAPHIES AND A WORLD BEYOND POLICING

Celeste Winston

Duke University Press   Durham and London   2023

Printed in the United States of America on acid-free paper ∞
Project Editor: Livia Tenzer
Text design by Matthew Tauch
Cover design by A. Mattson Gallagher
Typeset in Alegreya and Degular by
Westchester Publishing Services

Library of Congress Cataloging-in-Publication Data
Names: Winston, Celeste, [date] author.
Title: How to lose the hounds : maroon geographies and
a world beyond policing / Celeste Winston.
Other titles: Errantries.
Description: Durham : Duke University Press, 2023. | Series:
Errantries | Includes bibliographical references and index.
Identifiers: LCCN 2023008323 (print)
LCCN 2023008324 (ebook)
ISBN 9781478025313 (paperback)
ISBN 9781478020509 (hardcover)
ISBN 9781478027430 (ebook)
Subjects: LCSH: African Americans—Segregation—Maryland—
History. | Community organization—Maryland—History. |
Police-community relations—Maryland—History. | Discrimi-
nation in law enforcement—Maryland—History. | African
Americans—Social conditions. | Racism—Maryland. | African
Americans—Violence against. | Police brutality—Maryland. |
Police abolition movement. | African Americans—Civil
rights—Maryland—History. | Police misconduct—Maryland. |
Maryland—Race relations—History. | BISAC: SOCIAL SCIENCE /
Ethnic Studies / American / African American & Black Studies |
SOCIAL SCIENCE / Human Geography
Classification: LCC E185.93.M2 W567 2023 (print) |
LCC E185.93.M2 (ebook) | DDC 975.2—dc23/eng/20230503
LC record available at https://lccn.loc.gov/2023008323
LC ebook record available at https://lccn.loc.gov/2023008324

Publication of this book is supported by Duke University
Press's Scholars of Color First Book Fund.

It is a fact which I have never been able to explain, that there are those whose tracks the hounds will absolutely refuse to follow.

Solomon Northrup, *Twelve Years a Slave* (1853)

Contents

Acknowledgments

I am deeply grateful for the people who gave me the inspiration, support, and encouragement that brought me to the culmination of this book. Based on my research at the Graduate Center of the City University of New York (CUNY), *How to Lose the Hounds* reflects the community that has grown around me across years.

Ruthie Wilson Gilmore helped guide me to this research through a fortunate series of encounters that began before I met her. As a first-year undergraduate geography student, I read her book *Golden Gulag: Prisons, Surplus, Crisis, and Opposition in Globalizing California*, which opened my mind to thinking about practices and landscapes of confinement and ways to organize out of them. About four years later, I had the privilege of becoming a student of Ruthie's at the CUNY Graduate Center. Many of my ideas for this project were shaped through Ruthie's teaching and guidance. Ruthie, I am forever in gratitude for the time that you spent helping me think expansively and materially about racial capitalism, state violence, experience and consciousness, abolition, and so much more. You have taught me to work and write with a fierce care for storytelling in service of liberation.

To Katherine McKittrick, thank you for inviting me to consider why and how the concept of marronage resonates with me, to ethically attend to the historical present of slavery and its geographic legacies, and to submit to the exciting and bold Errantries book series at Duke University Press. To Marianna Pavlovskaya, I am grateful for your guidance on mapping and considering gender and care work in my discussion of community safety and security. Robyn Spencer, I am thankful for your advice to give deeper attention to the historical conditions and the collective memories shaping Black communities in Montgomery County. Thank you all for your generous readings of and feedback on my research, and for doing the disruptive and transformative work that has created space in academia for work like mine.

My book is shaped by additional feedback, stimulating questions, and support that I received from many other scholars along the way, including Richard Wright, George McDaniel, Naomi Murakawa, Kevin St. Martin, Bryant Simon, Judith Levine, Mona Domosh, Ajima Olaghere, Danya Pilgrim, and my colleagues at Temple University and the CUNY Graduate Center. Thank you, all. Earlier versions of chapters 2 and 5 benefited from suggestions I received at workshops held by the Department of Geography at Dartmouth College and the Public Policy Lab at Temple, respectively. I want to give special thanks to my two anonymous reviewers for devoting valuable time to make this work better, and to my editor Rose Ernst for helping me sharpen my writing and consider the reviewers' feedback in new and helpful ways.

I also want to acknowledge the folks at Duke University Press who helped me bring this book to print. I am particularly thankful for my phenomenal acquisitions editor, Courtney Berger; editorial associate Laura Jaramillo; books managing editor Liz Smith; project editor Livia Tenzer; and Errantries series editors Simone Browne, Deborah Cowen, and Katherine McKittrick.

My research has also been supported by generous grants and fellowships from the Graduate Center of the City University of New York, the Office of the Provost and the Public Policy Lab at Temple University, the Social Science Research Council, the Beinecke Foundation, the Institute for Citizens and Scholars, and the American Council of Learned Societies.

To the people in Montgomery County, Maryland, who made this research possible—thank you. Archivists Sarah Hedlund at Montgomery History, Pat Andersen at the Jane C. Sween Research Library, and the folks at Peerless Rockville and the Kensington Historical Society enthusiastically helped me locate the archival texts that enabled me to tell the story in the ensuing pages. To the community members whom I interviewed, thank you for sharing your stories and your own personal archives with me. I am honored to have been in conversation with you. I want to especially express my appreciation for the late Sharyn Duffin, the late Gwen Reese, and the late Warren Crutchfield. I am filled with gratitude for the time I shared with these unforgettable community elders before their passing. Local historians Sharyn Duffin and Gwen Reese worked to uphold a rich intellectual tradition of honoring Black life and community making that helped guide me from the archives to local Black community members. Warren Crutchfield connected me with people to interview, checked in with me during my fieldwork and writing, and made me laugh by refusing to call me anything but Dr. Winston even before I got my PhD.

Finally, my family has been a grounding force for me throughout my life. To my parents—Kim, Walter, and Sharon—thank you for supporting and celebrating me. Thank you also to my siblings, niece and nephew, aunts and uncles, and grandparents for your warmth and love. Going back home to the Washington, DC, metropolitan area to do my research felt good because of you all. To my partner, Jalil, thank you for loving me, living life with me, bringing me joy, and challenging me to think deeply about my work and to give my mind time to rest when needed. Thank you for listening to both my joyful and my anxious monologues about research and writing, and for reading and commenting on my work with care. This book is as much yours as it is mine.

....

Parts of the introduction and chapter 2 have been revised from "Maroon Geographies," *Annals of the American Association of Geographers* 111, no. 7 (2021): 2185–99.

Prologue

> When blackness, black human life, and the conditions imposed upon it enter discussions ... what does this then do to those very discussions?
>
> **Simone Browne,** *Dark Matters: On the Surveillance of Blackness* (2015)

Run!

During the small hours of February 1, 1942, on Baltimore, Maryland's thriving Black entertainment corridor along Pennsylvania Avenue, a group of people gathered around a young Black man and urged him to flee from a police officer. The man—twenty-six-year-old Thomas Broadus—was a soldier from Pittsburgh stationed at Fort George G. Meade in Maryland after being drafted into the army in 1941. That night in Baltimore, he had attended a Louis Armstrong performance with three companions.

Following the performance, Broadus and his group were stopped by white police officer Edward Bender. Their "crime" was attempting to hail an unlicensed, Black-operated taxi. Bender demanded that Broadus's group seek service from a white-owned taxi company instead. Broadus protested this police interference, arguing that he "wanted a colored cab and had a right to spend his money with whomever he chose" (*Afro-American* 1942). In response, Bender apprehended Broadus and began beating him with his nightstick.

Get away!

Broadus initially managed to break loose of Bender's wrath with the support of the crowd. Through radical feminist acts of care, several women helped free Broadus from the blows Bender wielded with his nightstick. One woman even took off her shoe to use it to beat the police officer (*Afro-American* 1942). With significant injuries inflicted by Bender's nightstick,

Broadus was only able to walk, not run, away from his attacker. While Broadus struggled to take steps away from Bender, the officer shot him in the back. Reeling from the pain of being shot, Broadus then tried to take cover under a nearby parked car. As he crouched down, however, Bender shot Broadus in the back a second time and compounded the injury of the gunshot wounds by repeatedly kicking Broadus. When some witnesses volunteered to transport Broadus to a hospital, Bender threatened to shoot them as well (Y. Williams 2015). Thomas Broadus was ultimately placed in a police car and taken to the city's only Black-serving hospital, where he was pronounced dead five minutes after being admitted.

Edward Bender was initially charged with murder and later found not guilty by a grand jury (Baum 2010). The jury reversed its decision to indict after meeting with the Baltimore police chief. An official statement from Bender's police captain justified Bender's use of excessive force with claims that Thomas Broadus had grabbed Bender's nightstick and struck the officer with it several times on the head before running away (*Afro-American* 1942). The statement also claimed that Bender's first shot that night was fired in the air and that he only fired one shot at the soldier, despite the hospital staff finding two bullet entry wounds in Broadus's body among the other injuries inflicted by Bender (*Afro-American* 1942). Bender was never prosecuted (Baum 2010). This was his second killing; he had killed a twenty-four-year-old Black man named Charles Parker in 1940 (*Afro-American* 1942).

In the wake of Thomas Broadus's murder, a group of about two thousand Black protesters marched to the Maryland state capitol at Annapolis on April 23, 1942, to demand an end to police brutality. Speaking on behalf of the protesters, W. A. C. Hughes Jr., attorney for the National Association for the Advancement of Colored People (NAACP) and a leader of the Citizens' Committee for Justice, denounced the routine police violence in Baltimore.[1] He argued that "liberty, the pursuit of happiness and even life itself is seriously jeopardized in the city of Baltimore by the totally indifferent and frequently oppressive action by police officers." He went on to point out that since Baltimore police commissioner Robert F. Stanton took office in 1938, "there have been ten killings of colored citizens by policemen." Hughes cautioned that "a serious racial conflict may result unless some remedial steps are taken."

It is telling that the "remedial steps" laid out presaged the types of reforms suggested today when police killings occur. For example, Hughes called for "a full and complete investigation" of police abuse charges by "a special committee of outstanding citizens" appointed by the governor. In addition, believing that racial diversity in police departments would help bring an end to police brutality, protesters requested that Black police officers be hired in Baltimore. Along those lines, the Reverend Eugene W. White, secretary of the Citizens' Committee for Justice and pastor of Providence Baptist Church in Baltimore, stated: "One of the greatest needs of our racial group in Baltimore is colored policemen in uniform to assist in upholding the laws, preventing crime and running down criminals. Baltimore has only three colored policemen who are not, and never have been in uniform."[2] Other requests included the appointment of a "colored magistrate" in Baltimore and the hiring of a second policewoman to the Baltimore police force. Protesters' demands also addressed much broader needs for more employment opportunities and Black representation in state and local government (Shoemaker 1994).

As a routinely unimaginative conclusion of highly contested police cases, a committee was formed. During the twentieth century, committees and commissions on race and civil rights became a common institutional response in the United States to quell Black rebellion without resolving its root causes (Hinton 2021). The April 1942 demonstration in Annapolis, along with meetings with Black leaders, prompted Maryland governor Herbert R. O'Conor to appoint an interracial commission "to study problems affecting Maryland's Negro population," including police relations (Governor's Commission on Problems Affecting the Negro Population 1943). After convening for months, the subcommittee on problems involving the police recommended the following:

1   That a copy of the Commission's report on "Questions Affecting the Police" be sent to the State's Attorney with the request that the Bender case be again sent to the Grand Jury.

2   That a copy also be sent to the Commissioner of Police with the request that appropriate charges against Officer Bender be formulated and tried by the Commissioner in his authority as head of the force.

3   That the Commissioner of Police appoint a colored police woman at an early date.

4   That one or more of the Negro policemen on the force be assigned to the duty of patrolmen in uniform.

5   That worthy young colored men be encouraged to prepare themselves to pass the examination and to secure places on the eligible lists.

6   That an amendment of the law relating to the Board of Police Examiners be sought, so as to secure the appointment of non-partisan examiners with long tenure in office.
(Governor's Commission on Problems Affecting the Negro Population 1943)

Following these suggestions, the Baltimore police department appointed the city's first three uniformed Black police officers (Y. Williams 2015). By 1950, Baltimore's police department had hired fifty Black police officers (Baltimore City Police Department, n.d.). Other reforms made in Maryland since then to combat racial police violence include diversity hires in police departments across the state beginning in the 1950s, community policing initiatives beginning in the 1980s to encourage police officers to become more familiar with their enforcement areas and collaborate with local residents to prevent and target crime, a 1995 agreement by the Maryland State Police (MSP) to end racial profiling (following a class-action lawsuit brought against MSP by the American Civil Liberties Union), a 2001 law requiring racially disaggregated data collection on traffic stops in Maryland, and a 2009 law requiring Maryland law enforcement agencies to report data on their use of Special Weapons and Tactics (SWAT) teams.

From the 1943 Governor's Commission to today, however, the State of Maryland and City of Baltimore have failed to resolve the issue of police violence. A case in point is the widely publicized and protested death of Freddie Gray on April 19, 2015. The murder of Freddie Gray occurred just days before the seventy-third anniversary of the protests surrounding the police killing of Thomas Broadus. Gray's death was the result of coordinated violence by six Baltimore police officers who, similar to the officer who killed Thomas Broadus, were either acquitted or had the charges against them dropped before going to trial.

In addition to the parallel between such tacit acceptances of police brutality spanning more than seven decades, there is commonality in the method of struggle taken up by Broadus and Gray. Like Broadus, Freddie Gray ran from the police when he was stopped. Possibly with his mind flashing through memories of his past arrests, Gray took flight with another man after a police officer made eye contact with them (*Baltimore Sun* 2015). These shared moments of Black flight across time are a central focus of this book. What happens when we understand the stories of Thomas Broadus and Freddie Gray not only for the losses of Black life they tell but also for the kinds of "life and living memory and whatever is in between"

(McKittrick 2021, 106) that emerge out of Black flight from policing? How can a retelling of police brutality through the framework of Black flight serve not as a descriptive rehearsal of anti-Black violence but instead as a lens into how we can "live with our world, differently, right now and engender new critical interventions" (McKittrick 2021, 139)? These questions mark a critical departure from the inertia characterizing the policy arena surrounding policing, wherein the prevailing queries already assume policing to be an answer to the "problem" (Du Bois [1903] 2015) of Black people and Black geographies.

Typical of this inertia, some of the same steps and policy recommendations made following the 1942 killing of Thomas Broadus were put forward in the wake of Freddie Gray's murder. For example, the Maryland Senate president and House speaker created a Public Safety and Policing Workgroup in May 2015 to address issues of policing following Gray's death. Similar to the Governor's Commission on Problems Affecting the Negro Population organized in 1942, this work group recommended that recruitment standards be evaluated and modernized to increase the presence of women, African Americans, Latinos, and other minorities in law enforcement departments (Hughes, Gruber, and Rossmark 2016). This call echoed demands for more racial and gender diversity on the Baltimore police force seven decades prior. But as the racial and gender backgrounds of the police officers responsible for Gray's murder make clear, diversity cannot resolve the issue of police brutality: three of the six officers were Black, one of whom was a woman.[3] The State of Maryland, like the rest of the United States, has proven unwilling to turn away from ineffective, stale reforms in efforts to address police violence. The long appeal of police reform reflects enduring institutional priorities across the political spectrum to legitimize the police function in enforcing the inequality and oppression integral to the development and maintenance of racial capitalism in the United States (Center for Research on Criminal Justice 1977; Maher 2021).

The state's responses to the police killings of Thomas Broadus, Freddie Gray, and the countless others whose lives have ended at the hands and weapons of police officers in the United States are deeply inadequate. Rather than quelling the violent operations of the police state, reforms set forward often focus on suppressing the fire of Black rebellion through crisis and diversity management. In addition, solutions presented for the problem of police brutality routinely involve deeper entrenchment of police presence in communities; for example, some community policing reforms even include incentives for officers to live in the areas they police. These liberal reform approaches incorrectly "identify policing as a fundamental tool of law and order that serves the collective interests of society, and locate the problems of police in a failure to adhere to constitutional law" (Akbar 2018, 410). The consequences of this reformism include ongoing state and state-sanctioned racial violence. Instead of further investments in policing, what is needed is a turn to "nonreformist reform," which Ruth Wilson Gilmore explains as "changes that, at the end of the day, unravel rather than widen the net of social control through criminalization" (2007, 242).

In the pages that follow, I present a Black geographic history of non-reformist approaches to combatting police violence. The places where I have gathered histories and present-day stories of such approaches are rooted in the same type of defiance called for by the crowd gathered around Thomas Broadus on that winter night in 1942 and carried out by Freddie Gray in 2015: Black flight. Moreover, while it is unknown whether Louis Armstrong learned that Thomas Broadus lost his life to a police officer that night after his performance in Baltimore, Armstrong himself sang of flight from police later in his career:

> Pops, did you hear the story of long John Dean?
> A bold bank robber from Bowlin' Green
> Was sent to the jail house yesterday
> But late last night he made his getaway . . .
> While they offered a reward to bring him back
> Even put bloodhounds on his track
> Those doggone bloodhounds lost his scent
> Now nobody knows where John went
> (Louis Armstrong, "Long Gone")

Louis Armstrong's lyrics, onlookers' exhortations for Thomas Broadus to flee in 1942, and Freddie Gray's flight from police in 2015 all demonstrate that policing is a deadly force from which to escape, not a system to invest hope and resources in correcting. Such refusals of policing invite a new type of analysis that does not simply interrogate the most brutal excesses of state power but instead points toward a way out of quotidian state violence by centering radical possibilities embedded in struggles for Black life.

While this prologue centers the historical geography of Black flight in Baltimore, the book now pivots to Montgomery County, Maryland—an equally important geographic site about forty miles from Baltimore and nestled against the northwestern boundary of the US capital, Washington, DC. At the same time that critical struggles against police brutality in major cities like Baltimore have shaped much of the police reform debate in the past century, Black geographies at other scales and places pose significant geographic confrontations with and possibilities beyond state and extralegal racial violence. We can locate Montgomery County in a diaspora that includes the nearby city of Baltimore along with other places formed through Black flight and placemaking. Within this diasporic framework for Black struggle, expanded scalar and political potentials result from engaging and recognizing places like Montgomery County: "spaces that are not normally celebrated—or even noticed—in our present geographic order" (McKittrick 2021, 182).

Alongside Thomas Broadus and Freddie Gray, who attempted to save their lives by fleeing from police, the people whose stories have shaped my writing carry a Black geographic tradition of flight that informs their organizing against and outside police surveillance and control. Their stories—and their accomplices in flight—reveal fissures in the law enforcement apparatus as well as everyday strategies of care and fugitivity that refuse, disrupt, and elude policing. It is my hope that these strategies help the reader imagine how safety can and must be ensured without police.

Introduction

How to Lose the Hounds: Maroon Geographies and a World beyond Policing is a guide to police abolition. It asks how *marronage*, the practice of flight from and placemaking beyond slavery, anticipated future Black refusals of policing. In answering this question, the book centers Black communities that have been subjected to violent excesses of police power from slavery until the present day. These communities demonstrate long-standing and ongoing ways to secure public safety and well-being without police.

The long history of Black subjection to police brutality might suggest looking beyond Black spaces for alternatives to police. In well-meaning arguments for defunding the police, for example, several prominent organizers, scholars, and politicians—including Mariame Kaba, Alex Vitale, and Congressperson Alexandria Ocasio-Cortez—have pointed to affluent, white suburbs as models for police abolition.[1] This approach is correct in asserting that abolition is already practiced in our world. Yet, as Tamara K. Nopper (2020) asserts, "abolition is not a suburb": while affluent, white suburban neighborhoods offer alternatives to police and incarceration, these spaces lack meaningful structures of accountability and harm reduction. Moreover, the very maintenance of affluent, white suburbs is predicated on the exclusion and policing of working-class people and people of color. Thus, solutions to police violence cannot involve turning away from Black spaces and toward such dominant geographies. It is precisely because Black communities are seemingly impossible sites for understanding life beyond policing that they provide critical lessons for why we must, and how we can, reimagine safety and community well-being without police. Black geographies show that abolition is "lived, possible, and imaginable" (McKittrick 2006, xii).

How to Lose the Hounds illuminates Black abolitionist placemaking from slavery through the present day. I explore what I call *maroon geographies*, which encompass sites of flight from slavery along with spaces of freedom produced through continuing Black struggles. Maroon geographies constitute part of a Black placemaking tradition shaped by subversions and rejections of dominant spatial imaginaries in addition to assertions of life-affirming forms of community. Across the Americas, marronage as flight from slavery took place during the sixteenth through nineteenth centuries. Through marronage, enslaved Black people asserted their freedom, evaded slave catchers, and created communities physically removed from the dominant slave society. Maroon communities ranged from small groups to large societies, and from "hinterland" to "borderland" groups that respectively settled deep in the wilderness or, conversely, near farms, plantations, and cities (Diouf 2014). Communities of maroons also became known by names such as *palenques* (e.g., in Cuba and Colombia), *cumbes* (e.g., in Venezuela), and *mocambos* and *quilombos* (in Brazil). Those who settled in maroon communities included Black people as well as Indigenous and poor white people excluded from slave society.

Much scholarship on marronage focuses solely on the historical significance and past cultures of these maroon communities and societies (Aptheker 1939, 1947; Price 1973, 1975, 1976; Leaming 1979; Agorsah 1994; Mulroy 2003; Leone, LaRoche, and Babiarz 2005; Thompson 2006; Diouf 2014; LaRoche 2014; Sayers 2014). Notable interventions include political scientist and Black studies scholar Cedric J. Robinson's *Black Marxism: The Making of the Black Radical Tradition* ([1983] 2000) and political theorist Neil Roberts's *Freedom as Marronage* (2015), which situate marronage within ongoing histories of radical Black struggle and theories of freedom that shape the past and the present. Following Roberts's (2015, 173) call for scholars to "reorient our epistemology of freedom around marronage," marronage has gained attention in scholarship on modern Black struggles and fugitivity (Joyce 2017; Quan 2017; Lebrón Ortiz 2019; Krueger-Henney and Ruglis 2020). I continue this work by expanding the temporal landscape of marronage to engage with its enduring legacies.

This book is principally situated in Black geographies scholarship, which examines the reverberations of transatlantic slavery in our current world order. This body of work contends that the slave ship, the auction block, the plantation, and other slavery-era geographies are ongoing loci of anti-Black violence and death in the Americas, reproduced in the present day through policing, imprisonment, immigrant detention, uneven development, environmental racism, and other systematic racial violence (Woods 1998; McKittrick 2011, 2013; Bledsoe 2017; Woods et al. 2017; Wright 2018; Vasudevan 2019; J. Davis et al. 2019; A. R. Roberts 2020). Black geographies scholarship also acknowledges how spatial acts of struggle and survival exist alongside and against the "historically present" geography of Black dispossession (McKittrick 2006, 7). As part of this research on persistent Black struggles against dominant geographies, geographers have stretched the concept of marronage to understand racial liberation struggles both in and beyond the spatial and temporal spaces of chattel slavery in the Americas (Bledsoe 2016, 2017; Malm 2018; Ferretti 2019; Thomas 2020; Wright 2020; Winston 2021). This geographic scholarship makes evident that marronage is an ongoing, expansive, and fundamentally spatial practice of building alternative worlds in service of liberation.

More than just a perpetual form of flight from unfreedom, maroon geographies encompass a method of *holding ground*: a geographic practice of making and sustaining place, and a refusal to yield, bend, or compromise in the face of attack or affront. In its noun form, holding ground refers to a "bottom that an anchor can hold in" (Merriam-Webster, n.d.)—which signals the often-invisible support structures undergirding sites of struggle and resistance. Holding ground contrasts with standing one's ground, a practice rooted in colonial dispossession and codified in stand-your-ground laws that legally permit people to use force (including deadly force) to defend one's self and property even when safe retreat is possible. Whereas stand-your-ground laws uphold centuries of racist legal doctrine that promotes violence for the sake of white property, holding ground is a care-filled practice of placemaking that transgresses dominant geographies. To hold ground is to engage in the "alternative ways of thinking about land use, stewardship, accumulation, and the environment" that are central to Black freedom (Hosbey and Roane 2021, 70). Thus, as a form of holding ground, maroon geographies underscore maroons' indelible impacts in a Black radical project of producing spaces that refuse to yield to racial violence rooted in the history and legacies of slavery. Maroon geographies demonstrate that freedom is not only a political horizon but is also an already extant place constructed through the work of oppressed people to organize land, social relations, and other resources for the purpose of liberation (Gilmore 2017, 227–28).

Maroon geographies form through Black spatial efforts to rework and reclaim geographic refuse: spaces that have been refused incorporation into dominant geographies and development, and sites where the people, land uses, and material environment are cast as marginal to the workings of racial capitalism's ecologies. During slavery, maroon geographies materialized in the spaces of swamps, mountains, forests, tall grasslands, and other "geographically difficult terrain" (J. C. Scott 2009, 6). The spatial features characterizing the so-called wilderness, such as "geographical inaccessibility, environmental detriment, [and] economic inefficiency" (Thomas 2020, 23), made such areas difficult for transformation by slave labor and thus untenable for inclusion in the racial capitalist plantation economy (Robinson [1983] 2000). Whereas land that was "not yet . . . subjugated to the rule of exchange-value" was considered "worthless waste" according to the logics of capitalism during slavery (Malm 2018, 11), it had long been invaluable to Indigenous groups inhabiting and caring for the land. Likewise, carrying their own "maroon ecology" (Malm 2018), Black people escaping slavery used this land as a critical basis for their flight to freedom from racial capitalism and the organized landscape of slavery. In Dominica, for example, the untamable forests beyond the coastlines became a "vast interior realm of maroon power where the whites dared not tread" (Malm 2018, 15). In the United States, the Great Dismal Swamp extending between Virginia and North Carolina was another site of geographic difficulty that enabled maroons to establish permanent homes beyond the confines of plantations. Where slavery took hold throughout the Americas, land subsumed into Western notions of wilderness became a premise, or necessary precondition, of freedom for maroons.

Since the abolition of transatlantic slavery, maroon geographies have continued to manifest through the reworking of a new form of geographic refuse. While most land previously considered to comprise the complicated category of "wilderness" has been tamed, occupied, or otherwise enclosed through colonization and racial capitalism—transformed into a "controlled, managed garden" (Merchant 2003, 389)—Black people continue to convert geographic refuse into "the cipher of a possible future freedom" (Malm 2018, 28). Modern maroon geographies manifest in "forgotten places" where "industries of last resort" like incarceration, oil refining, and waste management take hold while "real resolutions of economic, social, and technological problems" are "defer[red] to other places and times" (Gilmore 2008, 50). Such places, principally legible to capitalists through the register of abandonment, hold a capacity to generate new ways of life that push up against the constrictions of racial capitalism.

Contemporary sites of geographic refuse are conventionally referred to as spaces of white flight, deindustrialization, and environmental hazards without considering the ciphers of freedom created there. As racial conditions of slavery resonate in anti-Black violence today in "the context of persistent labor exploitation, hyper-surveillance, and unending incarceration," marronage continues through "border crossing, bench-warrant avoidance, and prison abolition" (Quan 2017, 184). Focusing on Black negations of policing's past and ongoing violence, this book underscores the wide span of slavery-era and more contemporary everyday Black abolitionist praxes.

A Brief History of Policing

Far from coincidental, the interconnections between Black abolitionist praxes rooted in past and present maroon geographies reflect the intertwined legacies of Black enslavement, slave patrols, and policing. In the United States, where much of this book is situated, the forerunners of modern police were known as slave patrols—or as "paddyrollers," "padaroles," "padaroes," and "patterolers" by the people they policed (K. Williams 2007, 36). Formalized in the US South at the beginning of the eighteenth century (Reichel 1988), slave patrols were employed by enslavers to maintain the dominant racial-economic order by capturing and punishing enslaved Black people who were found away from their enslavers' property without a proper pass. Patrollers also suppressed insurrections by disbursing unsupervised gatherings of enslaved Black people, searching Black homes for weapons, surveilling white people under suspicion of associating with Black people, and policing borders between "free" and slave territories.[2] Slave patrollers operated through violence, using an arsenal of guns, whips, binding ropes, and sexual assault to capture runaways and quell revolts (Wintersmith 1974; Hadden 2001). Slave patrollers' role in society was not to ensure public safety but to violently "maintain the racial and economic status quo" of slavery (K. Williams 2007, 66–67).

Slave patrol tasks were later folded into the duties of the nation's first police agencies. In southern cities, early law enforcement took the form of city patrols, guards, and night police tasked with punishing Black people traveling without passes or free papers, preventing gatherings of enslaved Black people, and generally targeting enslaved and free Black people with surveillance, harassment, and violence (K. Williams 2007, 41). Southern state laws limited or prohibited Black people from spending time in public spaces, being outside past specific times, carrying weapons, being "vagrants" (not having a job), trading goods with enslaved people, piloting a boat, preaching, owning dogs, seeking an education, writing or circulating books, and returning to a slave state after going to a nonslaveholding state (Dance 1987, 118).

Even in northern states, police agencies shaped their policing apparatuses to constrict the mobility and agency of Black, Indigenous, and mixed-race people, enforcing local racial laws as well as the federal fugitive slave acts (Campbell 1970; S. Browne 2015).[3] In the 1840s and 1850s, police forces in northern cities also adopted southern methods like wages and uniforms for patrolmen, and twenty-four-hour patrols (Rousey 1996, 14). Even prior to the legal authorization of their use of firearms, northern police officers armed themselves with guns following the southern example (Rousey 1996, 14). Tactics initially used to control enslaved people were being retooled in both the North and the South to selectively target and police a wider array of "dangerous classes" (K. Williams 2007, 75) composed of nonwhite people, poor white workers, and not-yet-white immigrant populations.

For descendants of enslaved people still living in southern states after emancipation, police continued to function during the 1860s through the early 1960s much as they had during slavery. For a Black person, post-emancipation-era interaction with southern police still meant the likelihood of violence coupled with a revamped form of forced labor. Police often used their power to force Black people into unpaid labor through convict leasing or chain gangs (Blackmon 2008). Black Codes, a set of laws passed by southern states between 1865 and 1866, buttressed convict leasing and chain gangs by criminalizing the same sort of everyday activities prohibited among Black people during slavery, such as loitering or breaking curfew. The result was the perpetuation of a southern labor economy built on the involuntary servitude of a swelling Black prison population, which surpassed the white prison population for the first time during the second half of the nineteenth century (J. Browne 2010). It took until the early 1960s—nearly a century after the abolition of slavery—for chain gangs to be abolished in every state (Lichtenstein 1996).

Today, police remain a key part of the US racial political economy by upholding a tradition of slavery-era policing technologies, practices, and imperatives. For example, police generate revenue for local governments through fines and court fees targeted at Black people. Municipalities with higher Black populations are more likely to take advantage of fines and fees as a major source of local revenue (Sances and You 2017). Police officers also continue to perform a type of "bodily surveillance" rooted in slavery (S. Browne 2015, 146), reading skin color, hair texture, forms of dress, and other biological and physical markers as indications of whether an individual threatens public safety and the dominant socioeconomic order. Moreover, many consequences of policing—mass "disenfranchisement, economic marginalization, and financial entrapment, including debt bondage and extreme social isolation"—are reminiscent of slavery (Quan 2017, 185).

The racial logics underpinning modern-day policing, however, resemble but "do not twin" the arrangements of slavery and the plantation (McKittrick 2011, 951). While policing traditions continue, they also evolve and operate in service of shifting goals. Police no longer function to support an economy based on Black involuntary servitude. Today, the majority of people incarcerated after being arrested by police spend their days incapacitated in public jails and prisons, neither working for free nor filling the coffers of private prison owners (Gilmore 2007, 21). According to the Sentencing Project (Buday and Nellis 2022), people incarcerated in private correctional facilities accounted for only 8 percent of the total US state and federal prison population in 2020. Moreover, as Ruth Wilson Gilmore (2017, 234) contends, struggles against mass incarceration can and should build, in part, on "the lineage of abolition extending through chattel slavery"; but "since half of the people locked up are not, or not obviously, descendants of racial chattel slavery, the problem demands a different explanation and therefore different politics" than a campaign to dismantle modern-day slavery.

Today's police suppress surplus labor to protect the current political economy rather than the slave economy of the past. Avery Gordon (2017) argues that policing has shifted from an overtly racial program of surveillance and punishment in service of unpaid labor to a system designed to preserve public order by isolating and disposing of threats to racial capitalism. These threats take the form of "surplus, disposable, and politically troublesome populations" that, in existence and through action, expose the fragility of our present world order and its organized failures to enhance political and economic freedom for all (Gordon 2017, 197). Groups disproportionately targeted by the police encompass working-class people, nonwhite people, immigrants, queer and nonbinary people, and people identified as mentally ill. The enduring racial codes operating today to justify this unevenness in policing include laws prohibiting drinking in public, possessing small amounts of drugs, making too much noise, and engaging in "disorderly conduct" (Vitale 2017, 31). Police enforce these laws through routine intimidation and violence, much like slave patrols and early police officers.

After centuries of advances and reforms, policing in the United States continues to share the same intrinsically violent nature of historical police apparatuses. In fact, while modern police departments stress their essential role in criminal justice and public safety, crime control remains just "a small part" of a policing system still centered on oppressive social control (Vitale 2017, 31). The danger that police disproportionately pose to poor people, people of color, people experiencing mental health emergencies, and people harmed by sexual assault is exacerbated by the idea that police protect these groups. On the contrary, police routinely respond to crises in these intersecting communities with inaction at best and with deadly force in frequent worst-case scenarios. For example, while a main justification for the need for police is to "prevent rape and arrest rapists," people who commit sexual assault "are rarely investigated, indicted, or convicted," and the police often inflict additional violence on survivors (Maher 2021, 53). Police also disproportionately use deadly force on Black Americans, who are three times more likely than their white counterparts to be killed by police; likewise, people with Latine, Indigenous, and Pacific Islander backgrounds are often twice as likely as white people to die by police brutality (Maher 2021). In addition, almost 25 percent of people killed by police in the United States in 2015 displayed signs of a mental health crisis (Saleh et al. 2018). The disproportionate policing of particular groups of people, however, is not the core issue; rather, abolitionists challenge the very act of criminalization that makes anybody vulnerable to the violence of the criminal punishment system in the first place (Gilmore 2016).[4] The persistent paradox of a system falsely purported to ensure public safety and security demands a conversation that moves beyond reform, one that extends abolitionist struggles dating back to slavery that have called for systematic flight from and refusal of policing all along.

Maroon Geographies and Police Abolition

Just as technologies of the slave patrol and early police preceded contemporary policing tools and practices, early Black struggles against policing anticipated later Black critiques and refusals of police (McKittrick 2011). In fact, contemporary organizing for police abolition—by groups like Critical Resistance; INCITE! Women, Gender Non-Conforming, and Trans people of Color Against Violence; Black Youth Project 100; and Black Lives Matter—build upon the political framing and imperatives embedded in historical struggles to abolish slavery. The movement for slavery's abolition was based on the understanding that abolition must encompass not only the end of slavery but also the creation of a new societal formation that dismantled and transcended the very logics upon which slavery was built (Du Bois [1935] 1998; A. Davis 2003). Similarly, police abolitionists work to end policing by developing and investing in completely different infrastructures that holistically support the safety and well-being of everyone.

Much of the everyday work of police abolition is carried out by Black folk who replace policing with care and accountability in their daily lives. Since the establishment of police as a central institution in US society, Black communities have negated policing as a system that routinely threatens and ends Black lives and, in its stead, created alternative models of safety and well-being. The long history of this practice, what I call an "everyday Black life of abolition" (Winston 2020), provides critical lessons for how we, as a society, can turn away from policing. As an ever-growing group of organizers, scholars, and political actors are embracing police abolition as a necessary and near political future in the context of pervasive anti-Black police brutality, I center maroon geographies as a vital model for police abolition. Following the lineage of Black texts that return to the past in order "to give blackness a future" (McKittrick 2021, 148), *How to Lose the Hounds* returns to historical geographies of marronage to show existing and possible future worlds of freedom from policing. A path toward police abolition need not be an imagined abstraction when it is evident in the archives, folklore, and ongoing life of maroon geographies.

A stirring example of an abolitionist praxis embedded in maroon geographies comes from the Gullah Coast region of the United States, spanning from Charleston, South Carolina, to Kingsland, Georgia. There, up until at least 1915, fugitives from the law avoided police capture using the same strategies as maroons. Anthropologist H. Eugene Hodges described their tactics in a short paper published in 1971 called "How to Lose the Hounds: Technology of the Gullah Coast Renegade," which inspired the title of this book. These fugitives—locally referred to as "renegades"—evaded the police by retreating to the swamps, forests, or offshore islands that had once provided shelter for maroons in the Lowcountry regions of Georgia and South Carolina. In order to throw the sheriffs' hounds off their scent, the renegades created false trails, rubbed wild onions or turnips on the soles of their shoes, kicked their shoes against skunks' bottoms, and used household goods such as red or black pepper, pine oil, turpentine, kerosene, and gasoline to destroy the hounds' sense of smell (Hodges 1971). Hodges attributes these methods for "losing the hounds" to Black people who had run away from rice plantations in the area.

In addition to fleeing from police, some maroons in the Americas developed their own justice systems and even continued their use after slavery ended. For example, the Djuka maroon society and the Matawai maroon tribe, both in Suriname, governed themselves with their own laws, at least until the tail end of the twentieth century (Köbben 1969; Green 1977). Each of these maroon societies, which "constitute the most enduring and oldest examples of continuous marronage" (Robinson [1983] 2000), settled the majority of their societal disputes without referring to Suriname authorities, even though Suriname state law technically applied to them. For example, the Matawais used communal councils consisting of elder men and women to adjudicate cases in which community norms were violated (Green 1977). These maroon justice systems continued to operate more than a century after slavery was abolished in Suriname in 1863 (Köbben 1969; Green 1977).

How to Lose the Hounds centers maroon geographies in Montgomery County, Maryland, as models for police abolition. Located in a border state between the Confederacy to its south and the free states of the Union to its north, Montgomery County served as an important site of the Underground Railroad during the American Civil War (1861–65). Many narratives of the Underground Railroad, including William Still's (1872) famous book on the subject, mention a route to freedom that Black people took into and through Montgomery County after traveling from Virginia, across the Potomac River and the Chesapeake and Ohio (c&o) Canal that divides Virginia and Maryland (Cohen 1994, 7). In *The Potomac*, a historical account of the Potomac River, Frederick Gutheim (1949, 105) recorded that above Georgetown and Great Falls in Montgomery County, "the river became shallower, islands appeared, and here and there were places where a man [sic] on horseback, or a pack train, could ford a stream." Fugitives from slavery traveling north on foot or by swimming also "sought out those areas of the Potomac which offered easy access into Montgomery County" (Cohen 1994, 7).

As another geographic aid to marronage, Montgomery County's rural terrain filled with fields of tall grass, thickets, and swamps enabled those fleeing slavery to conceal themselves "from the roaming patrols that travelled the public roads" (Cohen 1995, 324). Maroons could also follow various waterways in the county in their flight north. This physical landscape combined with the county's proximity to Pennsylvania to create a significant locus of marronage. For maroons escaping from enslavement in Montgomery County and beyond, the hope of freedom lay just forty miles north of the county in Pennsylvania, where the Act for the Gradual Abolition of Slavery was passed in 1780, slowly decreasing the state's enslaved population to zero by 1850 (Shaffner 1862, 252–53).

Marronage was thus a major ongoing practice in Montgomery County. The Maryland State Archives contain more than four hundred runaway ads posted by Montgomery County enslavers in local newspapers across the eighteenth and nineteenth centuries, before the state abolished slavery. The network of Black fugitivity in Montgomery County was so strong that enslavers throughout the region knew to trace the paths of their runaways there. For example, Thomas Hodgkin of Annapolis, Maryland, suspected that Frank, a man he enslaved, ran away in 1789 to Frederick or Montgomery County, where his "relations" lived (*Maryland Journal and Baltimore Advertiser* 1789). Likewise, Samuel Cissel of Clarksville in Howard County, Maryland, believed that Tilghman Johnson ran away to Sandy Spring in Montgomery County in 1859 (*Baltimore Sun* 1859). In 1845, W. M. Maddox of Washington, DC, believed that Maria, a woman he enslaved, was making her way north "through Baltimore or Montgomery county, or perhaps . . . on board of some Eastern vessel" (*Baltimore Sun* 1845). In 1857, an *Evening Star* newspaper correspondent in Washington, DC, attested to the geographic spread of fugitivity around the nation's capital: "It is quite certain that there are agents of the Underground Railroad at work in the adjoining counties of Maryland and Virginia" (*Evening Star* 1857). Maryland itself also became a final destination in many Black people's flights to freedom when the state abolished slavery on November 1, 1864, more than a year before the Thirteenth Amendment to the Constitution was ratified to officially abolish slavery across the United States.[5]

Black people who escaped or were emancipated from slavery as well as their descendants established more than forty Black communities in Montgomery County between the late eighteenth century and the late nineteenth century. Early Black residents took advantage of neglected and abandoned land—white society's geographic refuse—to create maroon geographies. By 1861, fifty-one Black landowners in the county owned a collective total of 17,142 acres (Afro-American Institute for Historic Preservation and Community Development 1978). These communities were often built on land deemed by white people as unworkable for living and farming due to its marshy or rocky conditions (Fly and Fly 1983). Among these communities, those established before the passage of the Thirteenth Amendment offered temporary and at times permanent safe havens for Black people fleeing slavery.[6] Likewise, Black people who established local communities in the aftermath of slavery continued building whole worlds from sites declared unfit for human life. These communities were, to a large extent, self-sufficient. Residents developed and maintained their own businesses and community institutions—generally churches, schools, and lodges or mutual aid societies. Their "impulse toward separatism . . . is rooted in maroonage and the desire to leave the place of oppression for either a new land or some kind of peaceful coexistence" (Kelley 2002, 17).

How to Lose the Hounds focuses on seven early Montgomery County Black communities: Sandy Spring, Haiti (pronounced "Hay-Tie"), Sugarland, Ken-Gar, Lincoln Park, Scotland, and Tobytown. Together, these communities offer portions of blueprints for an expansive project of police abolition rooted in maroon geographies. The communities of Sandy Spring, Haiti, Lincoln Park, and Sugarland have direct ties to marronage. In Sandy Spring, free Black residents, along with local Quakers (who began freeing people they enslaved around 1775), provided shelter to maroons traveling north to freedom. The history of Haiti (established around 1830) provides evidence of marronage as well: for example, records indicate that enslaved Black people fled from the area on the eve of the Civil War (McGuckian 1989). In addition, although Lincoln Park was not established until 1891, some of the first Black residents are believed to have escaped from enslavement in Virginia and West Virginia and settled in the community decades prior to its official founding (Eisman 1977). Likewise, local folklore indicates that prior to the official settlement of Sugarland by freed Black people in the 1870s and 1880s, fugitives from slavery were provided shelter in a cave and received financial assistance via a money line organized by local Black people (Gwen Reese, interview with author, December 13, 2017). In Sugarland, as well as Sandy Spring, Haiti, and Lincoln Park, marronage continued after the abolition of slavery through systems of care, protection, and collaboration that originally supported flight from slavery. In Tobytown (1875), Scotland (1879), and Ken-Gar (1892)—all communities formed after slavery—generations of residents also fostered spaces of trust and cooperation that reflect early maroon geographies. One of the key lasting impacts of this geographic history is a local terrain in which the violent logics and operations of policing are constantly interrupted and discarded in favor of established community support systems.

I locate the seven Black communities of Sandy Spring, Haiti, Sugarland, Ken-Gar, Lincoln Park, Scotland, and Tobytown within a network of maroon geographies. I do this to recognize their shared development along a spatial-temporal arc connecting flight from slavery to a broader

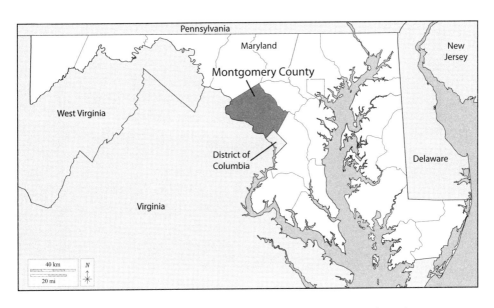

Map I.1 Montgomery County, Maryland, and surrounding states. Map by author.

geographic praxis of fugitivity through the twenty-first century. Maroon geographies exist not only where marronage is directly evident but also where its legacies can be found in folklore and examples of flight from racial violence more generally. This theoretical flexibility allows me to recast the margin—small Black suburban communities whose histories are mostly uncontained by the archives—as part of an "enlarged story field" (McKittrick 2006, xxix) of marronage and its afterlife.

Thus, this book demonstrates that just as marronage is itself a method of holding ground, the study of marronage demands a similar methodological approach. To hold ground methodologically involves rejecting conventional ideas of what counts as historical and geographic knowledge in order to recast marginalized historical geographies as part of a real, material basis for constructing places of freedom. What analytical possibilities are afforded by expanding how we define and delineate historical geographic practices? How might we include and center alternative knowledges as valid parts of the historical geographic record? What seemingly unlikely connections might be drawn across place and time through refusing the methodological impulse to exhaustively account for and document historical causality and continuity? In efforts to understand ongoing histories of

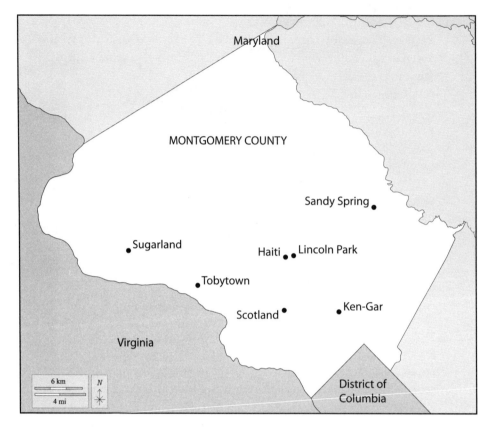

Map I.2 Black communities in Montgomery County study site. Map by author.

anti-racist organizing and placemaking, holding ground against the fore-
closures of conventional ways of knowing highlights the value and radical
promise of geography done differently.

Using the framework of maroon geographies, I aim to illuminate and
counteract the willful erasures of a thriving tradition of Black community
and fugitivity. In general, the prevalence of marronage has been frequently
denied or minimized in the United States by scholars. While many historians of marronage have devoted their attentions to the Caribbean and
Central and Latin America, marronage in the context of the present-day
United States has methodically been reduced to the actions of individuals called "fugitives," "runaways," "banditti," and "outliers" (Diouf 2014, 3).
Such atomization of the phenomenon of Black flight is partially a legacy
of white southerners who habitually disavowed the pervasiveness of Black

fugitivity and other threats to slavery. In contrast, I use the term *marron-age* to emphasize the systematic nature of Black flight from slavery and to connect sites of marronage in the United States to maroon communities across the Americas. Thus, *How to Lose the Hounds* is a project of what H. L. T. Quan (following Toni Morrison) calls "fugitive rememory" (2017, 182) as it re-remembers the history of Black communities, marronage and its carefully hidden legacies.

In building connections between marronage and the foundations for police abolition in Montgomery County's Black communities, this book asks three central questions: (1) What modes of safety and security did Montgomery County's early Black communities develop as alternatives and barriers to state and state-sanctioned policing? (2) How are definitions and practices of safety and security sustained across slavery-era and contemporary maroon geographies in Montgomery County? and (3) How do the social, political, and physical geographic arrangements of Black communities in Montgomery County model what Katherine McKittrick calls "more humanly workable geographies" (McKittrick 2006, xii), compared to the current terrain of policing? To address these questions, this book brings together historical and contemporary archival documents, including slave narratives, runaway slave advertisements, newspaper articles, police records, and the papers of local Black community institutions. To gain grounded information on local policing and Black placemaking beyond it, I also interviewed eighteen former and current residents of historically Black communities in Montgomery County. This approach offers a geographic perspective on the legacies of eighteenth- and nineteenth-century Black community organizing and their salience for Black abolitionist praxes today.

Nevertheless, I do not claim that Black communities operate uniformly and constantly in an abolitionist praxis or that Blackness is always aligned with abolition. Even in the Black communities that are the focus of this book, residents have varying and conflicting views and approaches toward policing. Across the United States, Black people have played a central yet complex role in shaping harsh US criminal legal policies over the past sixty years. With rising Black political power and numbers of Black elected officials, particularly following the passage of the Voting Rights Act in 1965, numerous Black leaders and their constituents advocated to secure what they saw as a historically denied civil right to access police and courts for their own safety; many also embraced "tough-on-crime measures" as part of efforts to protect the Black "community" from crime (Forman 2017, 11).

At the same time, Black rebellions took hold in every major US city between the mid-1960s and early 1970s to protest police brutality and broader systems of racism and anti-Black violence in the United States. In efforts to bridge the gap between formal politics and this direct action, Black elected officials spearheaded campaigns in the 1970s to bring housing, health care, welfare, schools, job training, and other social services to Black neighborhoods (Forman 2017; Hinton 2021). Black politics were thus animated by demands not only for police but also for other state resources denied to Black communities.

By the end of the twentieth century, however, state investments in Black communities mainly took the form of policing. In the 1970s and 1980s, austerity measures and the "war on drugs" in the United States operated in tandem to shrink budgets for social welfare programs and increase financial support for police intervention in Black and other marginalized neighborhoods. During this time, Black elected officials began supporting bigger police forces and increased police efforts to combat drug-related crises. For example, the Congressional Black Caucus sponsored the Reagan administration's Anti-Drug Abuse Act of 1986, which allocated $1.7 billion for the war on drugs and deepened racial disparities in policing and incarceration by establishing much harsher sentences for crack cocaine offenses than for powder cocaine (Taylor 2016, 100). During the 1980s and 1990s, many everyday Black folks also called for investments in policing to combat drug use, drug distribution, and intracommunity violence—all of which sparked anxieties in Black communities that were strategically appropriated by the state to rationalize the war on drugs (Murch 2015). The limited state-sponsored options for addressing drugs and violence, however, did not fully circumscribe Black neighborhoods. Even during crisis, Black communities like those in Montgomery County still provide a wealth of thoughtful and imaginative approaches to safety and security that do not always or solely rely on police.

The Story to Come

In the following chapters, I discuss how generations of residents in Montgomery County's historically Black communities have lived and continue to live out abolitionist praxes in their daily lives. Despite various social and economic pressures, including real estate development and speculation, urban renewal, rising property taxes, and demographic changes, some of these communities still survive or existed up until recently as enclaves of Black life. As part of ensuring their freedom, many residents of these communities developed alternatives and barriers to policing that still shape local maroon geographies. From outwitting slave catchers to not relying on police to resolve issues or ensure safety in their communities, the residents of Montgomery County's Black communities offer us already existing abolitionist praxes that can inform present and future attempts to abolish the police state. I center these communities' past and present placemaking and collective strategies of valuing their own humanity as a model for police abolition: the end of policing and the creation of new forms of safety and security.

Chapter 1 focuses on the history and folklore around marronage that have shaped and continue to shape Black communities in Montgomery County. From surviving tales of legendary escapes from slavery to continued ways of life, Black freedom still takes place as marronage. This chapter draws attention to important sites of struggle and connects the historical practice and the present-day remembrances and manifestations of marronage in Montgomery County. Further, I explore how Black community members' stories about their history are part of a larger Black folklore tradition around Black flight. I contend that the survival of this folklore has allowed Black community members to remain relatively conscious of enduring legacies of marronage.

Chapter 2 explores two local moments of flight from policing that occurred more than a century apart in the same location in Montgomery County. The first involves a group of maroons who confronted the county militia while traveling along a major county road in 1845, and the second focuses on a Black woman named Carolyn Twyman, a resident of Tobytown who refused to sign a ticket and fled from police officers on that same road in 1972 after they stopped her for a routine traffic charge. These two moments of flight from police create openings for reimagining a world beyond police. I also position Twyman's moment of flight as an extension of the "fugitive infrastructure" (Cowen 2017) of her neighborhood, Tobytown. Fugitive infrastructure supports ordinary people to organize and sustain life when possibilities for survival seem limited. Tobytown's fugitive infrastructure provides a lens through which to understand placemaking beyond policing as it took place during 1970s urban renewal.

Chapter 3 addresses what might fill openings left in the absence of police. I outline a model of maroon justice rooted in examples from Montgomery

County's Black communities and situate it in a broader discussion of restorative and transformative justice principles. Restorative justice encompasses coordinated efforts by groups of people to collectively repair relationships and restore peace following conflict and harm. Interlinked with restorative justice, transformative justice gives name to efforts by people to achieve broader collective liberation alongside restoring individual and community well-being. Examples of maroon justice in this chapter highlight the significant role of the Black church in resolving community disputes and issues, as well as a general practice among Montgomery County's Black residents of developing their own community-level forms of conflict resolution and definitions of justice.

Chapter 4 critically engages the ideal of "community" and the possibilities for developing radically unbounded practices of community that transcend conservative appropriations used to legitimize policing. The chapter interrogates the development of "community policing" beginning in the 1960s and focuses on ways that residents of Montgomery County's Black communities have defined community beyond policing. From their establishment, these communities have fostered a level of human connectivity and communal trust and care that often precludes their need to rely on police. Central to this chapter is a discussion of Black epistemologies and practices of community rooted in marronage and characterized by radical visions of and for spaces that fulfill human needs. These Black geographic visions show that community safety and security should be defined beyond policing. They also demonstrate that safety and security beyond policing mean something much more complex and far-reaching than simple one-to-one alternatives to state-based police and emergency response teams. It means turning away from police and turning toward community institutions of support and care.

Chapter 5 draws lessons from maroon geographies for abolition policy: plans and actions undertaken to produce a world without police. In an ongoing context of anti-Black state violence, I discuss how Black justice organizing can hold the state accountable outside of investments in existing state formations. Maroon geographies demonstrate how to move toward police abolition through both radical spatial transformations and strategic entanglements with the state. This chapter also explores how the commitments and goals of marronage are echoed in Black struggles against police violence in the United States and across the globe. Just as police have inherited a violent system of control and surveillance, the people who are policed have a geographic blueprint for fleeing and producing place beyond policing.

The epilogue concludes the book with a creative speculative vision for a world built on the absence of policing and incarceration and the presence of life-sustaining systems. This final story models how current and future liberation struggles might build upon the spatial artifacts and surviving geographic knowledge and practices comprising the sediment of unfinished "freedom dreams" (Kelley 2002).

1 Maroon Folklore as an Abolition Technology

Technology is the brilliance of making something out of anything, of making what we need out of what we had.
Alexis Pauline Gumbs, "Evidence" (2015)

In 2013, Maryland governor Martin O'Malley proclaimed November 1—the date that Maryland's state constitution abolished slavery in 1864—as "Maryland Emancipation Day" (*Senate Bill 42* 2013). This began an annual statewide tradition of programs, festivals, and exhibits held during the first weekend of each November to commemorate the end of slavery and historical struggles for slavery's abolition. As part of the 2017 Maryland Emancipation Day Celebrations, I went on a guided group hike of Montgomery County's Underground Railroad Experience Trail. The hike took place in Sandy Spring, an area known for its history of Black residents and Quakers harboring and assisting fugitives from slavery.[1] My group's "conductor" was a white former military officer who lives in Montgomery County. At the beginning of the hike, which started on a former farm that once operated on enslaved labor, the conductor pointed out our proximity to the Montgomery County Division of the Maryland-National Capital Park Police horse training facility. He warned us to keep our eyes out for police horse droppings that we might find scattered along the Underground Railroad trail. He then guided us along the trail, pausing at various points to share strategies that people fleeing enslavement used to avoid being caught, such as fleeing under the cover of a rain storm, traveling in forested areas, hiding and resting in prickly shrubs, using hollow trees as shelter, disguising themselves, and rubbing dung or onion on their shoes, clothing, or bodies. The conductor's warning to look out for physical traces of police presence as a preface to his account of flight strategies on the Underground Railroad is a symbolic reminder of the dialectical tension between marronage and policing. Black flight and police apparatuses have always coalesced as "a dynamic interplay between unified oppositions" (Baxter and Montgomery 1996, 8). Marronage asserts a demand for Black freedom and life, while policing operates as a direct negation of those assertions.

The history and folklore of marronage in Montgomery County show how refusals of policing took place in each act of flight from slavery, and in the assistance provided to maroons. Such refusals of policing, as this chapter and the chapters to come will demonstrate, have left indelible marks on the Black geographic landscape of Montgomery County. This chapter contextualizes local Black communities within a folklore of fugitivity and begins exploring some of the legacies of marronage in the communities of Haiti, Ken-Gar, Lincoln Park, Sandy Spring, Scotland, Sugarland, and Tobytown.

Maroon Folklore

Maroon folklore is a technology of escape that emerged during slavery to convey vital local knowledge about routes to freedom. Building from Alexis Pauline Gumbs's (2015, 39) definition of technology as "the brilliance of making something out of anything, of making what we need out of what we had," I consider maroon folklore a technology rooted in Black knowledges and practices of world building for the creation and maintenance of Black life. Stories about maroons gave hope to enslaved Black people and pointed them toward the possibility of—and methods for—their own escapes. This folklore of maroon fugitivity is part of a larger Black folklore tradition that connects marronage all the way to flight from prisons and the police state. As Daryl Cumber Dance (1987, xvi) argues, escape is "the oldest and most enduring theme in Black folklore and literature," which often recount escapes from enslavers, slave catchers and their hounds, sheriffs, the Ku Klux Klan, and prison. Dance goes on to argue that in the "Black folk lexicon, noted for its flexibility, its originality, and its vivid metaphors, there is no idea that has so many different words to express it as the idea of leaving, fleeing, running" (2–3).[2]

Maroon folklore is thus more than a cultural practice of storytelling about Black flight. Following the example of Clyde Woods (1998, 20), who theorized the blues as not only an "aesthetic tradition" but also an entire "theory of social and economic development and change"—what he termed the "blues epistemology"—I examine maroon folklore as a technology of Black placemaking. "Stories make place" and the acts of storytelling that produce Black geographies offer strategic lessons "in and for black life" (McKittrick 2021, 8–9). Understanding storytelling in this way reveals the unfinished nature of land; land is continuously shaped—landscaped—according to particular vantage points and aesthetics. While racist, sexist, and other dominating discursive traditions reflect and sustain prevailing landscapes, maroon folklore comprises a "poetics of landscape" (Glissant 1999, 150)—a set of creative acts that subvert dominant geographies and shape how we "organize, build, and imagine" our material surroundings as part of Black selfhood and community history (McKittrick 2006, xiv). Maroon folklore offers a vantage point from which to see the world differently and a practice by which to shape land according to visions of Black freedom.

Since the abolition of slavery, maroon folklore has continued to shape how residents of Montgomery County's historically Black communities define and struggle for Black freedom today. While local stories of flight from slavery have been transformed by the passage of time and transferals of oral history, they remain a bedrock of many Black residents' understandings of local Black placemaking. Former residents of Sugarland, for example, still discuss the history of resistance to slavery there. Black Sugarland-area residents are believed to have developed a "money line" during slavery through which people could leave money for fugitives to retrieve as they traveled toward freedom. Sugarland residents also allegedly hid up to twelve maroons at a time in a small cave, a secret entrance to which was built in a false floor of a local log cabin's fireplace (R. Davis 2008; Sugarland Ethno-History Project 2020). Across North America, caves were used to hide maroons—even Nat Turner sought shelter in a cave during the famous Nat Turner rebellion (Diouf 2014, 105, 280). Gwen Reese, who grew up in Sugarland, learned about these practices of fugitivity from other residents, and documented and preserved this history through the Sugarland Ethno-History Project, which she began in 2002.

In Sandy Spring, residents continue to carry knowledge of local historical ties with the Underground Railroad. After moving to Sandy Spring, for example, Paul Scott learned from his neighbors about local sites on the Underground Railroad. Likewise, Sandy Spring resident June Johnson told me that she has "always known that Sandy Spring was one of the legs of the Underground Railroad." In fact, her great-grandfather was born on the Woodlawn Manor estate, through which part of the Underground Railroad ran. His mother and father worked for the Palmer family, which owned

Woodlawn Manor between 1825 and 1919 (P.A.C. Spero & Company 1997). June Johnson and her family hold reunions at Woodlawn Manor because of their ties to the former Quaker farm.

Moreover, generations of residents have sustained knowledge of their personal ancestral connections to fugitives from slavery. In Lincoln Park, numerous residents have traced their ancestors in Montgomery County to the 1850s and early 1860s, when maroons began settling in east Rockville (Richardson 1988). One Lincoln Park resident, Evelyn Gaunt (1979), wrote of this early history in her notes for a local Black history exhibit in 1979:

> I've always heard my grandfather [Joseph Hicks] came to Rockville as a teenager, along with a friend by the name of Martin Broadnick [Broadneck]. They were escaping the effects of slavery. Maryland was a free state at that time. They are said to have swam the Potomac [River] from somewhere in Virginia.

For generations, descendants of the Hicks and Broadnecks have carried with them the history of the river escape, sharing oral histories about it with other residents.

In Sandy Spring, residents draw family connections to histories of marronage centering Enoch George Howard, William Henson Holland, Thomas John Holland, and local legend "Canada Jim." Enoch George Howard, who was manumitted from slavery in 1851 (Cohen 2006), is said to have housed Dred Scott while he awaited the decision of his 1857 Supreme Court case hearing, during which county resident and attorney Montgomery Blair represented Scott (J. Anderson 1999, 14). In addition to Scott, two brothers, William Henson Holland and Thomas John Holland, are also believed to have awaited the Dred Scott decision at Howard's home. They eventually fled to Canada when the decision went against Scott (Cohen 1994) and consequently upheld the rights of enslavers (even in free states) and denied the rights of citizenship to all enslaved people and their descendants (Library of Congress 2017). Likewise, James Wesley Hill became known as "Canada Jim" after he escaped to Canada from enslavement in Sandy Spring. Canada Jim repeatedly returned to local camp meetings—religious revivals organized by enslaved Black people—to entice potential fugitives to flee to Canada (Cohen 1995). He is believed to have led more than one hundred people to freedom beyond the Canadian border (Blankenheim 1985).

For generations, descendants of Canada Jim have practiced a rich oral history tradition to keep his memory intact. Sandy Spring native Alan Anderson, for example, was taught by his grandfather about the life and times of his own great-great-great uncle, James "Canada Jim" Wesley Hill. As an adult, Anderson recalled his grandfather telling him that enslaved Black people in the county used to whisper and sing about Canada Jim's impending arrival weeks beforehand (Blankenheim 1985). This folklore facilitated and simultaneously masked a local network of Black freedom. After slavery was abolished, folk tales about Canada Jim continued as a part of the local Black culture. Acting out how he imagined enslaved Black people to have communicated about Canada Jim, Anderson said to a local news reporter in 1985:

> Canada Jim is coming?
> Are you going with him?
> I don't know if I can, but I sure am thinking about it! (Blankenheim 1985)

Anderson's reenactment evidences the enduring connection to marronage that Sandy Spring residents hold and maintain through folklore.

The thriving oral tradition of marronage in Sandy Spring has enabled some residents to remain in contact with descendants of their ancestors who fled to Canada after escaping from slavery. Mable Thomas and her family in Sandy Spring hold biennial reunions with their family in Canada—all descendants of Enoch George Howard, William Henson Holland, and Thomas John Holland. These reunions of the Howard–Holland family, which began in 1992, have grown to as many as 450 people. The reunions are alternately held in Montgomery County or in Ontario, where William Henson Holland and Thomas John Holland settled (figure 1.1).

In addition to the surviving oral history tradition around and local connections to systematic flight from slavery, the folklore surrounding the naming of many Black communities in Montgomery County signals ties to slavery-era freedom struggles. For example, the community of Haiti—which was established during the 1830s—is thought to have been named after a practice of fugitivity from slavery. A local folk tale is that some fugitives from slavery were hidden in bales of hay in the area, therefore prompting the naming of the Black community there Haiti—pronounced locally as "Hay-tie." Others believe that the name Haiti originated from early Black residents' desire to draw a connection to the fight for independence among enslaved Haitians, whose 1804 Declaration of Independence officially declared Haiti as the new name for the French colony of Saint-Domingue ("Notes from Conversation with John Vlach" 1988). Across the United States, "Hayti" was a common name for Black settlements established in the nineteenth century, with the name even being used as a convention by mapmakers to locate predominately Black communities (J. B. Anderson 1990, 155).

1.1 "The Trek from Maryland to Canada." Illustration on display at the Sandy Spring Slave Museum and African Art Gallery, Sandy Spring, Maryland.

Similarly, Jerusalem (a Montgomery County Black community not in the main scope of this study) "is said to have gotten its name because it was used as a refugee camp for slaves escaping from Virginia during the Civil War—Jerusalem being 'the Promised Land'" (Soderberg 1992). An example from another area of Montgomery County is a community called Blue Mash, named after the dense marshy setting ("mash") where free Black residents of the community hid fugitives from slavery on their way north (Fly and Fly 1983, 36). Place naming by local Black residents is directly tied to a broader practice of renaming that was central to marronage (N. Roberts 2015). Maroons often gave new names to themselves and to the places that they chose to live in so as to set the ground for crafting new, free lives.

Even folklore about the naming of some local Black communities established after the abolition of slavery carries a similar tone of fugitivity. According to a local story, for example, the Scotland community got its name after residents seized a sign that read "New Scotland" from a neighboring property, painted over the "New," and posted the newly amended "Scotland" sign in their neighborhood (Levine 2000, 126). Up until around 1920, Scotland had been known as "Snakes Den"—named so because there were many snakes in the area; however, residents did not like the negative connotation of the name (Siegel 1973, 31). Their act of lawbreaking allowed them to define their own vision for their community and generated a new chapter of maroon folklore in Montgomery County.

Through the multigenerational transferal of such folklore about Black fugitivity, residents of maroon geographies in Montgomery County maintain understandings for how to create and sustain Black life and freedom in a world predicated on their negation. Framing maroon folklore as a technology helps locate marronage as an ongoing knowledge system for resolving everyday anti-Blackness. Technology is generally posited as the application of knowledge to solve everyday social problems, although dominant uses of technology systematically reify structures of racial violence and their attendant problems (Benjamin 2019). Dominant technology's role as a problem of anti-Blackness is evident in the history and aftermath of slavery—for example, through slave ships, slave patrols, police car dashcams, crime prediction algorithms, electronic ankle monitors, and airport security checkpoints (S. Browne 2015; Benjamin 2019). Less clear, however, is how a Black technology of abolition operates alongside these dominant technologies. In the following section, I discuss how Black folklore can be understood as a technology of police abolition.

Black Folklore and Police Abolition

The broader body of Black folklore in which Montgomery County's oral tradition of flight is situated reveals important lessons for how marronage can serve as a guide to police abolition. First, Black flight folklore can inform abolitionist praxes today through its celebration of disavowing authority. Some of the most popular figures in the Black folklore tradition are runners who are admired for their "absolute rejection of established authority figures—Ole Massa, the sheriff, the judge" (Dance 1987, 143). The trickster Brer Rabbit, as one example, makes trouble to survive and then hides out in briar patches. Stories about Brer Rabbit were shared by enslaved Black people and popularized more generally in early southern literature. Brer Rabbit tales not only challenged established limits of authority but also set new ethical boundaries, such as "friendship, altruism, and commitment to vulnerable members of the community," that were crucial for Black survival during slavery and its aftermath (Lussana 2018).

Later iterations of the Black anti-authority figure are fictional characters and real-life fugitives who literally and metaphorically run from the law. The character of Stagolee, based on a St. Louis pimp named "Stag" Lee Shelton who allegedly killed a man named Billy Lyons in an argument over a hat in 1895, is the subject of "more than 400 versions of the African-American folk song 'Stagger Lee,' as well as scores of books, academic theses and retellings on stage and page" (Hobart 2018). Many different versions of Stagolee's story exist, some of which reincarnate Billy Lyons as a white police officer whom Stagolee kills. Individuals like Assata Shakur, who escaped from prison and fled to Cuba after being falsely convicted of killing a New Jersey state trooper in 1973, are also venerated for running from the law. Stagolee and Shakur are regarded as part of a long tradition of Black fugitivity beginning with people like Nat Turner, Harriet Tubman, and Frederick Douglass. In fact, Assata Shakur (1998) herself famously proclaimed that she was "a 20th century escaped slave" in an open letter written from Cuba, which she called "One of the Largest, Most Resistant and Most Courageous Palenques (Maroon Camps) That has ever existed on the Face of this Planet."

Black folklore also demonstrates how to recast people beyond the distinction of innocence and guilt upon which the criminal legal system bases its existence. Black runner figures from slavery through the present day are respected in spite of and at times *because* of their lack of innocence as determined by law.

> One must remember that the Black runner, whether he or she be Nat Turner or Harriet Tubman or Frederick Douglass . . . or Stagolee . . . , is always labeled and regarded by the system as a fugitive, a desperado, a dangerous criminal, a vicious threat to society; and his [sic] flight is always in violation of the established law. . . . While on one level it may seem blasphemous to link the name of so valiant a heroine as Harriet Tubman with that of a cold blooded murderer, that chain was forged by their respective societies who judged them both the same and hunted them in like manner as similarly dangerous threats to the maintenance of order. (Dance 1987, 5–6)

The rejection of the false binary between innocence and guilt in the Black folklore tradition has roots in marronage. Since no fugitive from slavery was innocent—in the sense that they "stole" themselves away from their enslavers' keep—Black people from their beginnings in the United States had to define their liberation beyond narrow conceptions of innocence in the face of the law. Since slavery, Black communities have often continued to reject innocence as a guiding factor for granting freedom and life, and have developed their own boundaries of behavior and forms of accountability. These alternative measures form the basis of fugitive infrastructure and maroon justice, which I discuss in chapters 2 and 3, respectively.

Finally, Black folklore helps create the imaginative scaffolding necessary for police abolition across time and space. As a set of beliefs and stories told in a community across generations, folklore remains forever incomplete and unsettled. It is a combination of "myth, rumor, and story" (A. R. Roberts 2020, 215). In the space of unknowing, folklore offers a refusal of "the lawlike systems that underwrite the production of space; instead . . . hold[ing] in it the possibility of . . . a totally different system of geographic knowledge that cannot replicate subordination precisely because it is born of and holds on to the unknowable" (McKittrick 2021, 34). In the questions that folklore leaves unanswered, or the gaps in the story, sit an important invitation to imagine. How did these Black people escape enslavement and policing? What tactics did they use? How did they hold each other accountable? How did they remain safe in a world where police could not be called on? How can their stories guide continued struggles against state and state-sanctioned racial violence? In these unanswered questions lie possibilities for envisioning solutions that build on Black histories of struggle while not conforming to temporal and geographic limitations. Black fugitivity folklore can thus be understood as an "abolitionist habitus" (Schept 2015, 17): a generative structure, or grammar, for abolition within which infinite iterations of noncarceral practices and institutions are possible. In this way, Black folklore critically responds to the ways that carceral logics and practices reproduce themselves by transforming according to time and space.[3] Transforming alongside such carceral logics and practices, Black fugitivity folklore continues to offer innovative ideas for flight and placemaking beyond policing.

The linkages in folklore between Black flight from slavery and from prisons and police are not just metaphorical but also reflect material connections. The geographic history and folklore of fugitivity from slavery has played an integral role in shaping Black communities in Montgomery County. For example, one century after early Lincoln Park residents Joseph Hicks and Martin Broadneck fled from slavery across the Potomac River, the river remained a site of Black flight. Seymore Thomas, a resident of a local community named Martinsburg where freed Black people acquired land after the Civil War, is rumored to have helped a friend evade police capture after he was nearly apprehended for selling moonshine in the early twentieth century. The friend swam across the Potomac River from Montgomery County and sought asylum in Virginia when the local police closed in (Welsh 1961). Similarly, the Black community of Ken-Gar in Montgomery County was a popular site for people to flee arrests because, as county police Lieutenant E. J. Vaught said, the neighborhood "offers excellent opportunities for escape" due to its geographic isolation and single access road (Magruder 1976). The colocation of flight from slavery and flight from police across centuries in Montgomery County evidences the endurance of local maroon geographies.

A politics of marronage has successfully held strong in Montgomery County because marronage was characterized not only by flight from spaces of domination but also by placemaking. Marronage is a fundamentally spatial practice of building alternative worlds in service of liberation. Maroon geographies evidence "an ongoing black refusal of a passive relationship with space and place . . . [and] a dynamic interest in how geography is made and lived, through and beyond practices of domination" (McKittrick 2006, 92). In terms of developing a vision of police abolition, Black flight folklore illuminates how fugitivity can be a strategy of placemaking that offers refuge from the racially violent criminal legal system. In Montgomery County, the Black community-based oral history tradition around marronage undergirds multigenerational practices of producing relatively autonomous Black spaces. Black freedom continues to take shape in maroon geographies, wherein state violence is evaded through isolation, collectivity, and systems of care.

Black residents' "spatial self-affirmation and definition amidst an anti-Black society" (Bledsoe 2017, 44) is a central way in which they have continued to embody marronage in the postslavery era. In creating community on lands still reverberating with this history, early Black residents of Montgomery County strove toward autonomy and self-sufficiency. Like maroon settlements, Montgomery County's Black communities served as "fortress[es] [or] . . . haven[s] . . . from the hostile environment" surrounding them (McDaniel 1979a, 46). Many Black residents were able to buy land after emancipation—some even prior to emancipation—and formed tight-knit communities among themselves and other Black families to whom they rented (McDaniel 1979a). These unincorporated communities were, to a large extent, self-sufficient in various areas of life.

Residents built their own community institutions, including churches, schools, and lodges or benefit societies. Often, churches functioned at the intersection of these roles, serving as a religious institution, a site of children's education, and a meeting place for benefit societies and other organized groups. By the early twentieth century, approximately forty Black churches had been built in Montgomery County, with an average membership of about fifty people (*Community Cornerstones* 2014). As the heart of Black communities, churches expressed the community's moral standards, and church leaders often were empowered to approve or deny outsiders access to their communities (McDaniel 1979a). Churches provided a means to meet Black people's everyday needs, protect Black communities from outsiders, and even facilitate conflict resolution and harm accountability beyond the criminal legal system (this type of alternative justice practice is the focus of chapter 3).

The tight-knit, self-sufficient communities that Black Montgomery County residents formed enabled them to insulate themselves, in part, from racial violence on the part of the state and other dominating forces. Black communities were places of refuge from discriminatory housing practices; racially segregated schools, businesses, and public services; and racially targeted policing that characterized the suburbanization of Montgomery County following on the heels of slavery. Residents constructed their own homes, raised their own food and livestock, shared and bartered with one another, and provided each other with financial assistance, labor, and care work (McDaniel 1979a). They also established their own businesses, including general stores, bakeries, shoe repair shops, and beauty- and barbershops.

At the same time, local Black communities were sites of underdevelopment; many communities lacked some combination of heating, electricity, running water, sewage, and paved streets through the mid-twentieth century (Wiener 1977; Meyersburg 1978; Richardson 1988; Stieff 1991). Black communities were often excluded from, or on the losing side of, the development that brought Montgomery County its status as a wealthy suburb of Washington, DC. While the median family income in Montgomery County in 1959 was $9,382 (about 1.7 times higher than the national median family income of $5,660 at the time), residents of Black communities like Tobytown struggled to maintain year-round employment and lived in makeshift and dilapidated homes (Bureau of the Census 1961; City Planning Associates, Inc. 1969). The very underdevelopment of Black communities in Montgomery County facilitated the endurance of local maroon geographies.

In fact, maroon geographies exist through the reworking of geographic refuse—spaces that have been refused incorporation into dominant geographies and development, and sites where the people, land uses, and material environment are cast as marginal to the workings of racial capitalism's ecologies (Winston 2021). Black residents in Montgomery County's historically Black communities took advantage of the possibilities afforded by the underdeveloped, "geographically difficult terrain" (J. C. Scott 2009, 6) where they lived. The swamps, marshland, densely forested areas, and isolated places that offered temporary cover and long-term homes to maroons fleeing enslavement in Montgomery County had become Black communities with intractable barriers to outsiders. Residents of Black communities ensured their safety and maintained a sense of security through this lasting maroon tactic of isolation. Based on their seclusion and the strong ties they had with one another, they developed their own traditions and epistemologies of safety and security that centered themselves, rather than police, as safeguards in their communities. As a Haiti resident put it when I asked him if police patrolled his neighborhood when he was growing up, he responded with a laugh: "No, they didn't patrol our neighborhood. They couldn't even get up the road!"

In Lincoln Park, which was established where white folks dared not travel, residents saw opportunity in their marginality. Lincoln Park encompasses "a low, swampy area with poor soil" (Afro-American Institute for Historic Preservation and Community Development 1978, 36–37), divided from the rest of Rockville by railroad tracks on its eastern side, and bordered by a gas field to the north and industrial zones in all directions (Duffin 2001). Sharyn Duffin, a resident of Lincoln Park, explained the benefits of isolation:

> Since you're shut out from other places, you've got your own place to go to. It
> was shelter, and so you develop your own institutions. You don't have to deal

with the outside world, it doesn't want to deal with you either. So it was like a parallel culture. . . . It had its own protections. Everybody knew everybody, half of them were related. So if there were any strangers, you knew that immediately. There wasn't a whole lot of reason for any white folks to be wandering around either. So I guess that was the mindset the people had right along.

Similarly, Ken-Gar residents restricted vehicular access to their community to "only one way in and one way out . . . [which afforded] a certain amount of protection for blacks against the night riders of the day" (Flock-Darko 1992) (see figure 1.2). During the Ku Klux Klan's active reign of terror in Montgomery County, Klan members used to ride into the community and shoot bullets into the air to threaten Ken-Gar residents. Police rarely intervened. In fact, the Montgomery County Police Department went as far as openly supporting the KKK up until at least 1982, when the department protected the Maryland chapter of the Ku Klux Klan to "exercise their right to free speech" and worked to prevent the outbreak of violence after hearing that anti-Klan groups were planning counterdemonstrations at a Klan rally that year (Montgomery County, Maryland, Department of Police 1982). As Ken-Gar resident John Hopkins said, reflecting on the 125th anniversary of Ken-Gar in 2017: "Unless someone got shot or killed, the police weren't coming in here. . . . So there was always a feeling we were by ourselves" (Miller 2017). Hopkins's younger sister Doreen Hopkins Doye, who was born in 1956, recalled her father teaching her and her siblings how to shoot a shotgun in order to protect the family from the Ku Klux Klan. The family took shifts watching the window with a shotgun in hand, each sibling watching for about an hour at a time. "Thank God I never had to use it," she said (Miller 2017). Local Black communities' multiscalar self-defense efforts—ranging from individual home protection to restricted neighborhood access—exemplifies a broader spatial practice of Black self-defense that was vital to Black freedom struggles throughout US history. Even as Black people were legally denied the right to protect themselves from attacks by enslavers, white vigilantes, slave patrols, and police, they pushed back against anti-Black violence by harming and killing their enslavers, taking up arms against white vigilantes and slave patrols, and organizing movement groups like the Deacons for Defense and Justice (founded in Jonesboro, Louisiana, in 1964) and the Black Panther Party for Self-Defense (established in Oakland, California, in 1966) (Bledsoe 2021).

The self-defense efforts characterizing maroon geographies in Montgomery County connected local Black communities in a tight-knit social

1.2 "Ken-Gar: it likes isolation." From the *Montgomery County Sentinel*, March 25, 1976 (Magruder 1976).

network. In Sandy Spring, resident June Johnson explained that everyone living in her community knew the folks who knew where Sandy Spring was: "If you came out here, you were lost or invited. Many people did not venture past certain places out here in the country." In her community, residents felt a strong sense of safety for themselves and their families because they were able to sustain their own small world. As Johnson expounded:

> That's the one thing Black families have always done. They've always looked out for each other. Not just keeping your dwelling place safe, keeping your children safe. Keeping your environment safe. They looked out for your kids in the neighborhood. We ran all over the place here [as children]. My mother worked. My father worked. My grandmother was home, but other people worked. But people knew that the community was safe because Mama Lena was here, Miss Bernice was here, or somebody's home and the kids are not going to be lost. Somebody's watching out for them. That doesn't exist anywhere else except in the Black community, you know?

While Black communities across Montgomery County had strong ties with one another, they remained isolated from the surrounding predominantly white communities as well as institutions beyond their Black social sphere. This spatial isolation reflects both institutionalized racial segregation and the intentional efforts of maroons to build places of their own. Local maroon geographies have withstood time as a result of Black residents' continuous need to flee and create refuge from racial violence—from slavery to white vigilantism and police disregard for their well-being.

Over time, however, many historically Black communities in Montgomery County have disintegrated as a consequence of various social and economic pressures. Real estate developers, in concert with the local and federal government, bought up much of the land comprising Black communities (Porter 1988). A major wave of encroachment came during the 1950s and 1960s with real estate developers buying land to build white suburban neighborhoods and parks (Wraga 2001a). Another surge in displacement resulted from urban renewal projects in the 1960s through 1970s, whereby the lifelong homes of Black residents were cleared and replaced with a reduced number of public housing units for limited, carefully chosen residents to move back to their communities. This paved the way for further development to accommodate massive population growth in the Washington, DC, metropolitan area, where the total population was estimated at 3 million in 1969; that year, the area was projected to experience a three-fold increase over the next three decades, with suburban Maryland alone reaching 4.2 million residents by the turn of the century (*Washington Post* 1969). With increased property values and the building of townhouses and single-family homes surrounding Black communities during the 1980s, real estate speculators pressured Black residents to sell their homes by repeatedly calling and visiting with inquiries and offers to buy properties (Porter 1988; Rathner 2005). Industries have also contributed to displacement by building in historically Black communities. In the midst of industry encroachment and real estate development, older residents have passed away and much of the younger population has left for better access to employment opportunities and more affordable housing elsewhere. Other residents have been forced to move as a result of struggles to pay rising property taxes or due to zoning laws that prohibit any further subdivision of family property among descendants (Porter 1988). Once numbering more than forty, the Black communities established in Montgomery County between the late eighteenth century and the late nineteenth century have been gradually displaced and erased with this complex set of forces.

In spite of social and economic pressures and shifts, several historically Black communities still survive as enclaves of Black life. Descendants of some of the original residents of Haiti, Ken-Gar, Lincoln Park, Sandy Spring, Scotland, Sugarland, and Tobytown still live in or near these communities. June Johnson of Sandy Spring, for example, explained: "That's one of the things in Sandy Spring that's different from many of the other communities. The Black folks in Sandy Spring have held onto their land. They've not seen a need to sell it and make a dollar or whatever. All of these people that I've grown up with here . . . the families still own their land." As Johnson's quote suggests, sustained Black land ownership in Montgomery County has enabled some residents to maintain a world of freedom for themselves. Successful efforts by residents to hold on to their land through waves of urban renewal and industry and real estate encroachment demonstrate the liberatory possibilities that come to be when Black people have a place of their own. While the number of descendants of original residents has decreased and newcomers have moved in, several historically Black communities are shaped by a continuing geographic praxis of marronage.

Marronage in Montgomery County is the organizing basis for sustained local Black struggles against racial and economic violence. Black flight from and placemaking beyond this violence is both a persistent form of agency—"through which ordinary people organize to relieve the pressures that kill them and their kin"—and a resolute structure, or "residue of agency" held together by connection and remembrance (Gilmore 2008, 40). As the following chapters demonstrate, the enduring structure and agential practice of marronage in Montgomery County offer lessons for radically rethinking and reworking public safety beyond policing.

The Fugitive Infrastructure of Maroon Geographies

Marronage is not a metaphor. Running away is an act of survival and of literally making oneself unavailable for servitude and governing.

H. L. T. Quan, "'It's Hard to Stop Rebels That Time Travel'" (2017)

The history of marronage in Montgomery County, Maryland, shows how flight from slavery comprised—and directly anticipated later forms—of Black resistance to policing and law enforcement. Black people fleeing from slavery were always simultaneously fleeing from policing because law enforcement agents were tasked with capturing and imprisoning runaways or policing those otherwise deemed as threats to the institution of slavery. In fact, Montgomery County constables William Davis and Thomas Dawson were compensated for costs incurred by "suppressing tumultuous meeting of Negroes" as early as 1778, two years after Montgomery County's founding (Cohen 1995, 322). Likewise, Montgomery County sheriffs routinely pursued Black people who had escaped from slavery. Frequent notices in the *Montgomery County Sentinel*, a proslavery newspaper established in 1855 by County Sheriff Matthew Fields, "attest to the tenacity of the local sheriff in capturing blacks" (Cohen 1994, 28). In his newspaper, Fields regularly posted notices for enslavers of captured runaways to reclaim them.

In addition, the Montgomery County jail in Rockville, Maryland (which operated from 1801 until 1901), and the Maryland Penitentiary (which opened in 1811) imprisoned fugitives from slavery and those who assisted them.[1] Enslaved and free Black people alike could be jailed and then sold if they were stopped by the county constable and they were not claimed by an enslaver, could not prove that they were free, or were unable to raise jail fees ("An Act Relating to Servants and Slaves" 1676, 524). In addition, following the Nat Turner rebellion of 1831, the immigration of free Black people into Maryland was forbidden from 1832 until 1865; those who could not pay the fine demanded for immigration were sold to the highest bidder (Brackett 1890, 8). Thus, for free Black people, flight from policing and incarceration often meant flight from slavery, just as flight from slavery necessitated flight from policing and incarceration. In 1862, Maryland state law was amended so that enslaved Black people who were charged with offenses other than capital crimes (i.e., those for which an offender can receive the death penalty) could be imprisoned instead of sold or whipped (Brackett 1890, 8). Similarly, free Black people could be whipped or imprisoned instead of sold, and free Black migrants to Maryland could not be enslaved in the state for longer than two years. All "free black convicts" were still banished from the state upon release from the penitentiary "under penalty of sale for a term as long as they had been imprisoned" (Brackett 1890, 8).

Even as Maryland legislators took steps to abolish slavery, they reinforced linkages between Blackness, enslavement, and incarceration. The 1864 Maryland Constitutional Convention, in which slavery was abolished in the state, was shaped by claims based in biological determinism about Black people and their ability to lead upstanding, productive lives following emancipation. For example, Isaac D. Jones, a former US congressmember from Somerset County, Maryland, argued that abolishing slavery would "plunge this unfortunate class [of emancipated Black people] into idleness, crime and degradation" (qtd. in Hemphill 2020, 181). Moreover, Black people who had suffered the consequences of laws concerning slavery were forced to continue living out their sentences in prison. During the constitutional convention, "a motion to provide for the liberation of all persons imprisoned under laws arising exclusively from the institution of slavery, was lost by a tie vote" (Brackett 1890, 8). This effectively kept intact direct linkages between slavery, policing, and incarceration for years to come.

As a counterpunch to the enduring bond between the abolished institution of slavery and the US criminal legal system, marronage continues to live on as an important infrastructure of Black fugitivity. Infrastructures, generally defined, are material systems that organize and sustain everyday life (Cowen 2017). While physical "systems of highways, pipes, wires, or cables" make up what is commonly understood as infrastructure, people themselves can also be considered infrastructure, as they intersect and collaborate with one another to reproduce life (Simone 2004, 407). Thus, in their flight from and placemaking beyond slavery, maroons themselves

People are a type of infrastructure

formed a type of infrastructure. Marronage materialized into—and continues to structure—what Deborah Cowen (2017) calls "fugitive infrastructure": material arrangements produced through cumulative efforts by everyday people to organize and sustain life when possibilities for survival seem foreclosed. Emerging in opposition to auction blocks, plantations, slave patrols, and other infrastructures of chattel slavery, maroon geographies have always operated as a "furtive and tenuous infrastructure" encompassing the material conditions of Black refusal (Roane 2018, 256). In the post-slavery world, the fugitive infrastructure animating maroon geographies systematically pushes back against the power and ongoing violence of anti-Black infrastructure.

The language of fugitivity, in relation to infrastructure, illuminates how everyday survival acts often deemed unlawful can combine into a material basis for struggle. In maroon geographies, fugitive infrastructure forms through Black people's creative work—often bordering on the "extralegal" or "criminal"—to "sustain living in the context of intermittent wages, controlled depletion, economic exclusion, coercion, and antiblack violence" (Hartman 2019, 237). The disregarding of such work as aberrant and criminal has facilitated systematic disavowals of a robust fugitive infrastructure undergirding Black geographies. Across the history of marronage in North America, this has occurred through white efforts to deny the existence of marronage and to atomize Black flight from slavery with terminology such as "runaways," "outliers," and "banditti" (Diouf 2014, 3). Far from disconnected, however, the acts of Black flight and survival that shape maroon geographies consolidate into an entire infrastructure.

Fugitive infrastructure delineates an organizing framework through which to comprehend people's adaptability and reactions to oppressive structures not as isolated and individual but as equally structural as the structures they resist. In formulating what she calls "abolition geography," Ruth Wilson Gilmore (2017, 238) asserts that "feeling and agency . . . [are] constitutive of, no less than constrained by, structure." While dominant structural forces like slavery, urban development, policing, and incarceration certainly constrain human life and agency, everyday people also systematically build fugitive infrastructure against and outside the "space, time and legality" (Cowen 2017) of these dominant infrastructural projects. This is not to say that people's daily decision-making may be predetermined by the fugitive infrastructures that might organize their lives. Rather, fugitive infrastructure lends coherence to the unbounded ways that "ordinary people and communities assert their own renderings of life and living rather than those of the state, capital and other dominions' terms of order" (Quan 2017, 178).

Fugitive infrastructure has shaped Montgomery County's maroon geographies for centuries, despite attempts by police and representatives of the state and federal governments to snuff it out through control, displacement, and development. To illustrate the endurance of fugitive infrastructure shaping maroon geographies, this chapter overlays three stories of marronage and policing in Montgomery County that took place between the mid-nineteenth century and the late twentieth century. The first story features a troop of maroons who attempted to evade capture while traveling through the county in 1845, making their way north to freedom. The second case of marronage centers around a Black woman named Carolyn Twyman, whose refusals of policing during the 1960s and 1970s brought her in direct connection with the path to freedom taken by the troop of maroons more than one hundred years prior. Finally, the chapter concludes with a discussion of Twyman's community of Tobytown, where residents resisted the criminalization of their neighborhood amid an urban renewal project during the 1970s. In tying together these stories, I explore past and future possibilities afforded by maroon geographies characterized by fugitivity in the face of these projects of state violence.

First group to boldly walk through town to [...]

1845: A Troop of Maroons

In July 1845, a group of about forty maroons swiftly marched through Montgomery County on a journey to Pennsylvania, approximately forty miles north of the county. Armed with various weapons, ranging from butcher knives and swords to pistols, they were prepared to fight for their freedom to the death. They traveled openly in daylight along Frederick Road (what is today Maryland Route 355) in rows of six (Meyer 2018). In reference to their bold escape attempt, the *Montgomery Journal* remarked: "This is the most daring movement which has ever come under our observation. We have heard of gangs of negroes travelling through parts of the country sparsely inhabited, but never before have we heard of their taking to the public road in open day within 2 miles of a County town, and in a thickly settled neighborhood" (*Montgomery Journal* 1845). About two miles north of Rockville, Maryland—the Montgomery County seat—on Frederick Road, the fugitives were confronted by a county militia called the Montgomery Volunteers, and a group of citizens recruited to help by Sheriff Daniel Hayes Candler (Meyer 2018). Upon this confrontation, the leaders of the maroons called on the group to "resist to the last," and a number were able to flee and were never captured (*Montgomery Journal* 1845). Thirty-one members of the group, however, were apprehended and confined in the Montgomery County jail. One of the leaders—a free Black man named Mark Caesar—was among the captured and subsequently tried and convicted "as a free negro aiding and abetting slaves in making their escape from their masters" (*Port Tobacco Times, and Charles County Advertiser* 1845). He was sentenced to forty years in jail, where he died in 1850 (*Port Tobacco Times, and Charles County Advertiser* 1850). Another leader of the group—an enslaved man named Bill Wheeler—was able to flee from the confrontation but was eventually arrested and convicted, receiving a life sentence in prison. Four months later, he escaped from jail and was never apprehended (*Port Tobacco Times, and Charles County Advertiser* 1846).

This historical case of marronage emphasizes the intertwined history of flight from slavery and flight from policing. The forty maroons' pursuit of freedom required them to challenge the state through their collective violation of laws forbidding flight from slavery. While the majority of the group was apprehended, their uptake of weapons against the Montgomery Volunteers and the county sheriff's recruits—in broad daylight, no less—demonstrates their disregard for the state's claim on the "monopoly of legitimate physical violence" within its bounds (Weber 1994, 310–11). In this way, the unachieved freedom for most of the group still provided a stark challenge to policing. Moreover, taking place sixteen years before the start of the US Civil War, this bold act of resistance evidenced a growing Black insurgency that helped lay the foundation for future struggles to end slavery. By challenging state law and violence along a public road, the troop of maroons bolstered a Black fugitive infrastructure that "disrupted and remade" the ways in which power organizes "time, space, and the material world" (Spice 2018, 47).

This example also highlights the almost paradoxical nature of fugitive infrastructure. Whereas infrastructure signifies permanence and rootedness in place, fugitivity implies that which is in flight, fleeting, transitory, or temporary (Spice 2018). The seemingly impossible overlay of these multiple characteristics invites a consideration of what it means to produce a material, grounded basis for flight. Can resistance in the form of escape lend itself to sustained infrastructural placemaking? Maroon geographies evidence the capacity of Black flight to produce long-standing, multigenerational infrastructures that disrupt dominant power structures and relations. While not causal, the relationship between these fugitive infrastructures and Black flight have persisted over time and scale, across local geographies.

1972: The Crisis of Carolyn Twyman

More than a century after the group of forty maroons traveled northward to freedom and fought against local authorities, the same road in Montgomery County again became a locus of Black flight from policing. In September 1972 in Rockville, Maryland, a Black Tobytowner named Carolyn Twyman refused to sign a ticket and fled from a police officer when he stopped her for what was described as a routine traffic charge. After refusing to sign the ticket, she was reported to have cursed at the officer and driven off in her car at a speed of thirty-five miles per hour, making her way northward on Maryland Route 355—traversing the same path that the maroons had taken 127 years prior, and passing by the former county jail where they had been detained. After she fled from the officer, a police dispatch was broadcast indicating that a "Negro" or "Colored" woman driving a Chevy had refused to sign a ticket and was fleeing (Wims 1973).[2] At the height of the chase, Twyman was pursued by nine police cars, some of which were traveling at speeds of more than one hundred miles per hour. To avoid capture, Twyman changed direction at various points, increased her speed, and even cut across an empty parking lot when a Rockville City Police car attempted to block her in (see map 2.1). Twyman drove a total of three and a half miles before she was killed in the chase, her car having flipped over after striking a metal pole.

The story of Carolyn Twyman's flight from police alongside the historical case of marronage highlights the spatial and functional overlap of policing and incarceration across the era of slavery and the present day. While Twyman's flight took place in an automobile, the ongoing policing of Black mobility links her story with that of the maroons before her. These examples also make clear how challenges to policing across that same stretch of time and space are interconnected. In both cases, the actions of Black freedom seekers revealed and created ruptures in geographic arrangements of racial governance. The maroons shocked local white residents by eschewing

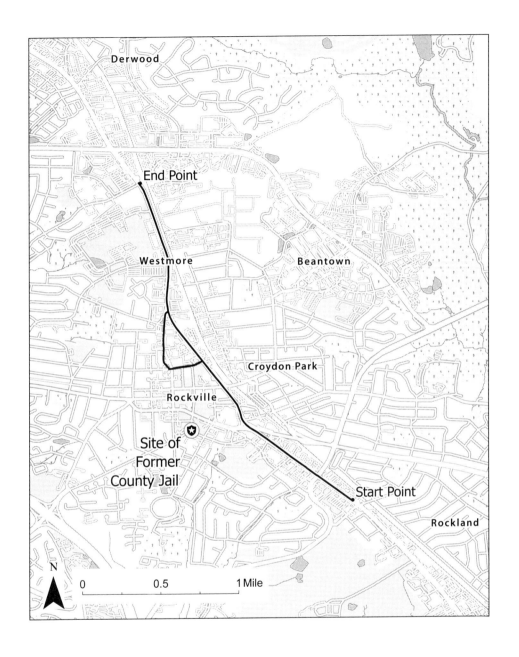

Map 2.1 Carolyn Twyman's flight route in 1972. Map by author.

the convention of traveling a sparsely inhabited path at night and instead taking to a public road in daylight through a densely settled county town on their journey to freedom. Similarly, in fleeing police along that same route, Carolyn Twyman effectively threw the police into crisis by publicly disrupting their authority and sense of control—which led to a violent police chase that ended in people questioning the very role and logic of policing.

At the scene of Carolyn Twyman's crash, more than two dozen people gathered and questioned why nobody was helping her—one of whom was Miss Mary Green, a friend of Twyman. Green, who remained at the scene of the accident until the ambulance took Twyman to the hospital, reported that the officers present were "standing around and talking about their personal matters" and that "nobody was trying to get Mrs. Twyman out of the car until the ambulance arrived" (Wims 1973, 3). Green stated that she attempted to get closer to Twyman's car when an unidentified officer told her to get the "fuck" back or she would be arrested (Wims 1973, 3). Another witness at the scene stated that "the police were very rude" (Wims 1973, 4).

After Carolyn Twyman's death, her brother—also of Tobytown—contacted William G. Wims, a Black member of the Montgomery County Human Relations Commission, to ask if the true story behind the incident could be ascertained. He believed that his sister may have been set up because she had filed a police brutality suit against the police force after a conflict with police seven years prior. In that case, she had been trying to dispose of her old car by setting fire to it when the police and fire department approached her to put the flames out. She protested and the police handcuffed her and beat her, during both her arrest and her time in police custody at the Montgomery County Police Station. When she was pulled over by the police seven years later, Twyman had been steadily arguing her police brutality case in the courts of Montgomery County. It is likely that the police chase was thus, in part, a consequence of the police department's frustration with Twyman's ongoing challenge to their authority. Allegations were made that one police officer had even threatened "to get" Carolyn Twyman before her death (Montgomery County, Maryland, Department of Police 1972, 1).

Commissioner Wims answered Twyman's brother's call and presented a motion to his fellow commissioners to request a full investigation of the incident by the State Attorney's Office and the State Human Relations Commission. In a report presented during a Human Relations Committee meeting before the motion vote, Wims pointed out that "it is against police policy to chase another auto for a violation. Therefore, [he questioned,] why did nine police cruisers chase this 'Colored Lady' who was black and proud of it?" (Wims 1972). The motion also included requests for the officers involved in the chase to be suspended with pay pending full investigation and for human relations training to be increased for all police officers. These requests reflect the predominant centering of police professionalization as the most effective strategy to combat anti-Black police brutality in the United States (Hinton 2021). Regardless of the conclusion of the investigation, the potential remedies proposed could not have prevented future police violence. Officer suspensions—with or without pay—and increased human relations training for police officers are reforms that operate through the false idea that police brutality is an aberration in an otherwise working system.

Commissioner Wims's motion—which passed, ten for and one against—failed to establish a comprehensive investigation of Twyman's case. While the police colonel agreed to supply the Justice Committee and Human Relations Commission with a report on the incident, the police department conducted the investigation through its own Internal Affairs Division and did not suspend the officers during the investigation. In addition—like countless federal, state, and local government human relations commission reports that pathologized Black people in response to the demands of 1960s and 1970s Black urban uprisings against police violence (Hinton 2021)—the investigation worked to criminalize Twyman. One of the main forms of justification given for her death was an official police report indicating that she had a blood alcohol content reading of 0.14 percent—suggesting her judgment and motor functions were impaired—despite witnesses' stories that suggest Twyman had only consumed half a can of beer that day. This justification for Twyman's traffic stop was just one of almost endless possible narratives used to apprehend Black people for "driving while Black." Regardless of any violation a police officer may point to, "it is race more than legally justifiable probable cause that most often provides pretext for car searches" (Bloch 2021, 142) and ultimately structures the car as "a primary site of carcerality" for Black people (Bloch 2021, 148).

Despite the police department's initial erasure of race as a cause for the policing of Carolyn Twyman, Commissioner Wims was hopeful that the results of the internal police investigation would prompt the Human Relations Commission to conclude that the officers racially discriminated against Twyman. He strongly suspected that racial discrimination was at play in Twyman's death: "If I were not trying to be neutral and let my blackness help me answer the questions, I would answer yes, the Montgomery

County Police Department discriminated against Mrs. Twyman" (Wims 1973, 7). Despite his personal analysis of Twyman's death, Commissioner Wims (1973, 7) acceded to the procedural terms of the investigation: "Being neutral, and looking at the facts given to me, I must say that although the Police Department made many mistakes, I can't reach this conclusion alone, but must rely on the decision of the entire Commission."

Ultimately, the Commission voted to ignore any evidence of racial discrimination in the case. On February 26, 1973, about four months following Carolyn Twyman's death, the Justice Committee released the following statement: "The investigation of the . . . case conducted for the Committee and the Commission . . . has not disclosed evidence of racial discrimination in connection with the death of Miss [redacted] during a police chase. The Committee is of the view that the case has been adequately investigated and that further investigation is not justified. Accordingly, the Committee recommends to the Commission that this case be closed" (Justice Committee 1973, 1–2). The Human Relations Commission had decided that Twyman's postmortem future would be closed for further public scrutiny and grievance.

In fact, many of the archival documents pertaining to Twyman's case were still access-restricted by the Human Relations Commission when I visited the Montgomery County Archives in 2018. Along with Twyman's case, other restricted Human Relations Commission Justice Committee files included a 1957 accident between a white driver and Black driver, who felt police were disrespectful during their response to the accident; a police shooting in Lincoln Park in 1967; a 1973 meeting on police–community relations between the Human Relations Commission and the Montgomery County Police Department; and an investigation into an attempted escape from the Montgomery County Detention Center in 1973. To access the restricted files, I had to pay a charge of fifty cents per page for an archivist to photocopy the original documents, redact any personally identifiable information, and rescan the documents for my viewing. The resulting documents (see figure 2.1, for an example) were peppered with black blocks obscuring the names of all people involved. This act of redaction marks the state's systematic, "willful absenting of the record" (S. Browne 2015, 2) in order to conceal threats to its police apparatus. Due to the simultaneous inclusion of nonredacted, unrestricted files in other Montgomery County Archives collections, however, I was able to identify all individuals included in the Human Relations Commission reports on Twyman's case (figure 2.2). The unfinished censorship of Twyman's story denotes the impossibility of

⑤-1

One week from tonight at approximately 11:50 p.m. Mrs. ███████
was killed in her auto while being pursuded by 9 different police
cars.

Mrs. ████ who approximately 7 years ago also was beaten while
handcuffed at the Montgomery County Police Station.

Mrs. ████ being raised in Tobytown tried to burn her own car which
was paid for. The police and the fire department wanted to put
the flames out while Mrs.█████ protested vigorously, at this point
the police beat her and fought her to the ground and legged and
handcuffed her. Once at the station she was hit over the head with
a steal handcuff. Medical detention was delayed for a couple of
hours.

She has been vigorously fighting in the courts of Montgomery County
trying to win a police brutality assault.

Last week after the police stopped her who knows what was said, all
that is known now is that she spead away from the officers. I
happen to be at a friends house that night listening to a police
radio when I heard an officer say a colored woman refused to sign
a ticket in persuit traveling north █████████* on route 355. *This was
Within a few minutes within a three mile stretch nine police   an existing
cruisers supposedly protecting the rights of the beloved citizens correction in
of Montgomery County were themselves breaking the law. Traveling   the document,
at speeds over a 100 miles per hous through the narrow urban streets not a
of Rockville it is a miracle that only one life was lost.   reduction
                                                                    - SH

Wednesday at approximately 7:30 a.m. Mr. ████ brother of the
Mrs. ████ called me and asked to see me. I went up to his home
in Tobytown and he asked me if I could get the Human Relations
Commission to help find out the true story behind the tragedy.
He asked me being a Commissioner if I could find out if they had
his sister set up because she had filed a police brutality persuit
against the police force. At this point Mr. ████ told me a
very unbelieveable truth, know police officer was at the hospital
to explain anything to the family, at this moment I do not think
the family has heard any from the police concerning the good
human relations, as a matter of fact I personally think that
Colonel ████ should have sent a sympathy card or flowers
to the family. I was also appalled that know one from any agency
excluding myself representing the Human Relations Commission
was at the funeral. The one exception being a community organizer
for the housing authority.

As I mentioned earlier it is against police policy to chase another
auto for a violation, therefore why did nine police cruisers chase
this "Colored Lady" who was black and proud of it. Why was there
know police officer at the hospital? What did the police officer
say to Mrs. ████ to make her run away?. Most important why did

2.1 Redacted Montgomery County Human Relations Commission report on the
police chase of Carolyn Twyman. Montgomery County Archives, Montgomery History, Gaithersburg, Maryland.

Mr. Wims presented the following report:

One week ago tonight at approximately 11:50 p.m., Mrs. Carolyn Twyman was killed in her auto while being pursued by nine different police cars. Mrs. Twyman, approximately seven years ago, had been beaten while handcuffed at a Montgomery County Police Station. Mrs. Twyman, who was raised in Tobytown, tried to burn her own car which was paid for. The police and the fire department wanted to put out the flames, while Mrs. Twyman protested vigorously. At this point, the police beat her and fought her to the ground and legged and handcuffed her. Once at the station she was hit over the head with a steel handcuff. Medical attention was delayed for a couple of hours. She has been vigorously fighting in the courts of Montgomery County trying to win a police brutality assault case.

Last week, after the police stopped her, who knows what was said? All that is known now is that she sped away from the officers. I happened to be at a friend's house that night listening to a police radio when I heard an officer say that a "colored woman" refused to sign a ticket in pursuit traveling north on Route 355. Within a few minutes, within a six-mile stretch, nine police cruisers supposedly protecting the rights of the beloved citizens of Montgomery County were themselves breaking the law, traveling at speeds over 100 miles per hour through the narrow urban streets of Rockville. It is a miracle that only one life was lost.

Wednesday, at approximately 7:30 a.m., Mr. Martin, brother of the Mrs. Twyman, called me and asked to see me. I went to his home in Tobytown and he asked me if I could get the Human Relations Commission to help find out the true story behind the tragedy. He asked me, since I am a Commissioner, if I could find out if they had his sister set up because she had filed a policy brutality pursuit charge against the police force. At this point, Mr. Martin told me a very unbelievable truth--no police officer was at the hospital to explain anything to the family. At this moment I do not think the family has heard anything from the police in the interest of good human relations. As a matter of fact, I personally think that Colonel Watkins should have sent a sympathy card or flowers to the family. I was also appalled that no one from any agency, excluding myself representing the Human Relations Commission, was at the funeral. The one exception was a community organizer for the Housing Authority.

As I mentioned earlier, it is against police policy to chase another auto for a violation. Therefore, why did nine police cruisers chase this "Colored Lady" who was black and proud of it? Why was there no police officer at the hospital? What did the police officer say to Mrs. Twyman to make her run away? Most important, why did the police pursue her at a high speed?

I think these questions merit the motion that I am about to present.

I move that the Montgomery County Human Relations Commission ask the State Attorney's Office to make a full investigation of this incident and report to the Human Relations Commission within 30 days. I also recommend that the 16 or so officers, including the officer who gave the other cars the order to pursue, be suspended with pay pending full investigation. We also demand that Colonel Watkins train every officer on the police force in basic human relations.

We hope that the word "colored" will never be used again by the Montgomery County police force.

To summarize, my motion is asking for three things:

1. Full investigation by the State Attorney
2. Suspension of officers with pay
3. Human Relations Workshops

The motion was seconded by Mr. Burke

2.2 Nonredacted Montgomery County Human Relations Commission report on the police chase of Carolyn Twyman. Montgomery County Archives, Montgomery History, Gaithersburg, Maryland.

complete state repression and the ability to read historical Black insurgency as a guide for ongoing freedom struggles.[3]

Carolyn Twyman's acts of refusal and flight from policing offer important lessons, rooted in marronage, for how to counter police violence. Her praxis of state evasion effectively threw the police into crisis by disrupting their authority and sense of control. In an attempt to suppress Twyman, the police actually compounded this crisis when nine police officers violated policy by chasing Twyman's vehicle and killing her. What can crisis tell us about the instability and therefore potential impermanence of police power? As H. L. T. Quan (2017, 182) contends: "People rendering themselves unavailable for governing trips up the system, more often than not, leading to crises of authority and further exposing elite incompetence and delinquencies. . . . The ungovernable withhold both consent and legitimation, and, in the process, render the state and its allies more transparently incompetent, brutal, and imperial."

The crisis surrounding the interaction between Twyman and the police led people to question the very role of police. For example, the twenty-five witnesses at the scene who critiqued the police officers' handling of the incident and Twyman's brother's questioning of the police officers' intent in stopping and chasing Twyman were products of the resulting crisis. These acts of questioning and sousveillance, a form of surveillance from below, are major parts of the process of abolition.[4] By making visible the violent power relations embedded in policing, these practices effectively produced a fault line in the terrain of police–state subject relations and thereby created a radical opening for alternatives to police.

In addition to prompting individuals to challenge policing, Twyman's death caused institutions such as the American Civil Liberties Union and media outlets to condemn the local police. Criticizing the police chase of Twyman, an article published in the local *Washington Area Spark* newspaper exclaimed: "The cops are dangerous enough with their clubs, blackjacks, and guns without having them racing around like maniacs in their prowl cars" (*Washington Area Spark* 1972b). *Spark* began in 1971 as a radical student newspaper at Montgomery College and grew into a working-class movement-based paper that pushed back against mainstream press, which *Spark* writers termed "the pig papers" (*Washington Area Spark* 1971, 8). In denouncing police violence, *Spark*'s coverage of Carolyn Twyman disrupted the media's traditional role of reproducing dominant ideologies around crime and order. While news stories about crime and victims of police brutality "are almost wholly produced from the definitions and perspectives of the institutional primary definers" such as police and courts (Hall et al. 1978, 68), *Spark* affirmed the perspectives of people like Carolyn Twyman, her brother, and the witnesses of her crash.

It is no accident that I chose to center a Black woman in my discussion of flight from police. In doing so, I follow Katherine McKittrick's "positioning [of] black women as geographic subjects who provide spatial clues as to how more humanly workable geographies might be imagined" (2006, xxiii). Twyman's story emphasizes that police violence is a systemic problem with wide-ranging consequences. Police brutality is not only an issue for Black men; it also impacts women and other groups of people who do not conform to societal norms. In fact, police have long "targeted sex workers and other women whose economic independence or free use of public space marked them as disorderly" (Hemphill 2020, 182). For example, during the 1860s through 1920s, vagrancy statutes made Black women particularly vulnerable to arrest for sex work, regardless of whether it was their first encounter with the law or if there was any proof of transgression (Hartman 2019; Hemphill 2020). For Twyman, the acts of setting fire to and later simply driving her own automobile marked her as errant, her free movements considered criminal acts. Black women like Twyman have long been targeted by police through racial profiling, sexual violence, and deadly and excessive force (Ritchie 2017). As Twyman's story demonstrates, police violence is also systematically justified by institutions purported to safeguard human rights like the Montgomery County Human Relations Commission. Institutional reforms to combat police brutality will therefore always fall short of a much more comprehensive project of police abolition.

Furthermore, Carolyn Twyman's story exemplifies the insurgent role of Black women in a long history of marronage. Her outward rejection of policing as well as the care work of her friend Miss Mary Green (whom the police also treated as a threat by profanely demanding that she step away from Twyman's crashed car) exist within a significant lineage of Black freedom struggles that have quite literally shaped the grounds upon which future battles are fought. The attempts by the group of witnesses to ensure Twyman's well-being and by Twyman's brother to publicize the truth behind her death are also located in a long-standing fugitive infrastructure that has supported acts of marronage across time. This infrastructure works to sustain Black life and freedom by challenging state authority and fostering a radical praxis of care in the face of state violence. Black care—

Her friend wanted to help but the police officer stood and watched and didn't let her help often led by women—during such struggles for freedom and life is a direct counterforce to the overwhelming violence of state force. It stands in juxtaposition to the state's inhumanity and, as a result, contributes to a breakdown in state authority and sheds light on a critical requirement of police abolition: that the end of policing be coupled with an attentiveness to human needs. When basic needs are prioritized above social control, the extraordinary violence of policing becomes unacceptable.

Moreover, Carolyn Twyman's death shows how often Black women's "spatial options are painful" (McKittrick 2006, 41) at the same time that they may allow them to "assert their sense of place . . . [and] manipulate and recast the meanings of . . . [dominant] geographic terrain[s]" (McKittrick 2006, xvii). For Twyman, flight from the police did not allow her to escape the fatal impacts of the racial and gendered violence of the state. Her death was another consequence of a long history of Black girls and women being marked and targeted by the state as being sexually deviant, of low moral character, overly aggressive, accustomed to violence, and implausible victims (Haley 2016; Jacobs 2017). These stereotypes originated centuries ago to justify Black women's enslavement and their exclusion from the protection of the law. The present-day outcomes of the state-sanctioned pathology of Black women include their disproportionate subjection to arrests, excessive force, sexual abuse, and killings by police officers.

Despite her being unable to completely upend the violent workings of the state, Carolyn Twyman's flight enabled her to dictate the terms and shift the geographic terrain of her struggle with policing. In the act of fleeing, Twyman was able to "jump scales" (Smith 1992, 60)—resisting police violence not just at the site of her body and her car but also throughout the street network of the Montgomery County seat. The scene of Twyman's Chevy Nova speeding ahead of multiple police cars chasing in pursuit, the news of her escape transmitted over radio waves, the audience that formed at the scene of her crash, and the subsequent investigation of the conditions of her death all worked to make her encounter with police violence a countywide rather than a solely individual crisis. As Gilmore explains, "crises are territorial and multiscalar" (2008, 32). The time and space of crisis surrounding Twyman's death echo the social and racial upheaval wrought by the troop of maroons in 1845 and similar historical threats to the institution of slavery. These crises also serve as windows into later clashes between Black fugitive infrastructure in Montgomery County and the agents and power structures of local government.

Physical/people infrastructure

Carolyn Twyman's community of Tobytown demonstrates how flight from carcerality takes place not only in direct encounters with police and state agents but through a broader infrastructure of fugitivity. Fugitive infrastructure in Tobytown manifests through creative efforts by Black residents to make life more bearable in the face of state abandonment and concentrated poverty. Tobytown, like Black communities throughout Montgomery County and the United States, developed with a deliberate lack of investment from public and private capital. For example, Tobytown lacked a trash collection service until around 1965 (Douglas 1965). Up until 1972, just one dirt street ran through the neighborhood (Bonner 1974), and most homes in the community lacked plumbing and electricity (Wraga 2003). The neighborhood was also isolated from public transit access to other parts of the county. In fact, just in 2016, after decades of residents pressing the county for better transit service, the Montgomery County Council approved a bus route that would service Tobytown (Shaver 2016). Prior to this, Tobytown's closest bus stop was "three miles away on a narrow country road with no sidewalks or paved shoulders to separate pedestrians from vehicles whizzing past" (Shaver 2016). This lack of transportation access made it difficult for residents to secure stable employment with livable wages (Bonner 1974). During the 1970s, Tobytown was known as "an isolated, poor community of blacks living in drafty, overcrowded shacks on a single dirt street, within sight of rich horse farms and rolling estates in Potomac, one of the wealthiest sections of Montgomery County" (Bonner 1974).

Tobytown residents, like members of other Black communities in Montgomery County, however, transformed this geography of public and private capital abandonment into a usable fugitive infrastructure. This infrastructure served to "creat[e] possibility in the space of enclosure, a radical art of subsistence" (Hartman 2019, 33). Early Tobytown residents constructed illegal affordable dwellings made of cinderblocks, wooden packing crates, corrugated iron, and other materials (Douglas 1965). Residents continued living in their homes despite twenty-three out of the neighborhood's thirty-five homes being condemned by 1964 (Wraga 2001a). In addition, in the absence of heat and plumbing, residents heated their homes using wood stoves in the winter, and they created a community privy. Through this material fugitive infrastructure, Tobytown residents were able to not only sustain life on the losing side of uneven capitalist development but also practice community on their own terms. They raised livestock, hunted small game, and grew their own produce in communal gardens. In addition, Tobytowners maintained a thriving neighborhood social life, which included criminalized activities such as gambling and public drinking. Their fugitive survival strategies also included burning their old cars to cheaply dispose of them—the cause of Twyman's arrest seven years prior to her death. Twyman's refusal of the policing of her car burning and her flight from policing seven years later was thus an extension of the fugitive infrastructure of her neighborhood. As chapters 3 and 4 will demonstrate, other Black communities in the county are similar spaces of fugitive infrastructure, where residents describe a long-standing tradition of eschewing police involvement in their communities.

The fugitive infrastructure of Montgomery County's maroon geographies is built not only through Black residents' systematic will to survive by defying dominant terms of social order but also through the consolidation of radically alternative norms, ethics, and support systems to govern their lives. For example, Black residents of Montgomery County organized mutual aid society chapters such as Rockville's Benevolent Society for the Black Community, officially chartered in 1912 as a local branch of the national Order of the Galilean Fisherman. This organization served as both a social space and a community trust for local Black people. George Meads, a resident of Haiti and one of the charter officers for this benevolent society, also led the first and only volunteer fire department in the county up until 1921 (Pathik 1975). This all-Black fire response team was established in 1895 and followed on the efforts of numerous Black men and women living in Rockville to extinguish fires throughout the town beginning in 1873 (Hedlund 2022). These early safety and support systems allowed Black residents to practice social reproduction despite state neglect.

In Tobytown, the community was kept secure not by police but by community members themselves. A former resident of the community Haiti, Annie Rhodes, recalled an old Black man who lived in Tobytown who used to sit on an overturned bucket at the entrance to his community to prevent intruders from entering. Upon Rhodes's first visit to Tobytown, the man got up from his bucket and walked up to the side of her car, and she had to explain to him her purpose for visiting and who invited her to visit. Reflecting on the encounter, Rhodes told me, "He was like their policeman." Rhodes explained that after she provided sufficient justification for her visit, the man said, "Go on by, lady," and she was told which house to go to. Every time Rhodes visited Tobytown afterward, she said, the old man was there, keeping guard. Tobytown's community-based security system is reminiscent of the Bear Creek maroon community, established in Georgia during the 1780s. This seventeen-acre settlement of approximately one hundred people was protected by a four-foot-tall breastwork that had a small opening to admit one person at a time (Diouf 2014, 198). In addition, Bear Creek maroons created a barrier of large trees to prevent boats from passing through the nearby creek, and they placed a sentry outside the settlement's borders (Diouf 2014, 198). Such defense measures were designed for the maroon community to protect themselves when attacked by militia troops. In Tobytown, the use of a similar system indicates the persistence of maroon epistemologies of safety and security across time and space. Maroon geographies are characterized by an ongoing rejection of state authority in favor of alternative methods to secure residents' well-being.

For generations, Tobytown offered Black residents a certain amount of protection and autonomy from the predations of a state and economy built upon racial violence. Even Montgomery County councilmember Elizabeth Scull recognized that Tobytown "'has been a symbol of security' for those in a surrounding world 'which has not been secure'" (*Tribune* 1972). Residents' protection and autonomy were largely secured through the illegibility and unapproachability of their community by outsiders. As James C. Scott (1998, 54) writes, "Historically, the relative illegibility to outsiders of some urban neighborhoods (or of their rural analogues, such as hills, marshes, and forests) has provided a vital margin of political safety from control by outside elites." It comes as no surprise, then, that when the local government in Montgomery County wanted to dismantle Tobytown's fugitive infrastructure, its efforts took place as an urbanization project, which is often designed to "simplify and rationalize the complex organic structure" of places in order to facilitate "circulation and access by agents of the state" (Freeman 2014, 31).

Urban renewal was one key way in which the local authorities attempted to constrain fugitive infrastructure in Tobytown and other Black communities in Montgomery County. It was the context in which Carolyn Twyman was killed. In the United States, urban renewal comprised a set of local and federal policies and programs designed to eradicate "blighted" areas from the built environments of US cities. Throughout the United States, more than two thousand urban renewal projects were implemented between 1949 and 1973, when the program officially ended. In the era of urban renewal, the term *urban* became less of a denotation of the scale and character of cities but instead worked as a signifier of race. In fact, urban renewal came to be known popularly as "Negro removal" because the projects were largely targeted at Black communities as a way to cement racial residential segregation. Nonurban Black spaces like the semirural suburb of Tobytown were also fair game for urban renewal.

Tobytown experienced preparation for urban renewal through the 1960s. This decade saw a growth in Montgomery County's population and increased pressure from development interests to expand middle-class suburban housing, parks, recreational spaces, and transportation infrastructure. In response to these shifts, Tobytowners increasingly faced threats to their land rights from developers and county officials. Elderly Tobytowner Robert Martin, for example, won a court suit and recovered his land after it had been taken from him through tax proceedings in the 1960s (Lippman 1967). Following the passage of the federal Housing and Urban Development Act of 1965, Montgomery County officials took advantage of new federal funding for housing programs and rent subsidies, expansion of water and sewer facilities, construction of community centers in low-income neighborhoods, and urban beautification. With assistance from these funds, Montgomery County worked to convert Tobytown "from a disgraceful rural slum into an attractive suburban community" (Eckardt 1967) by introducing trash collection, new privies, and a new pump for the neighborhood's main well prior to formally declaring Tobytown a renewal area in 1967 (Lippman 1967). As *Washington Post* correspondent Wolf Von Eckardt wrote of Tobytown's preliminary architectural design in 1967, "The way Rurik F. Ekstrom, the young Yale architecture graduate, working with planners Matz, Childs & Associates of Rockville, has designed the place, no Montgomery County home owner or zoner need fear for his property values." Instead of outright and complete erasure of Tobytown, Montgomery County officials could tap into federal funds to "clean up" Tobytown and appease Tobytowners' white, affluent neighbors.

In 1969, the plan for urban renewal in Tobytown was solidified. That year, a Montgomery County Community Renewal Program report (figure 2.3) was released, which identified Tobytown—along with almost all historical Black communities in Montgomery County—as "problem areas" plagued by "blighted housing, environmental blight, social disorganization, and poor community architecture" (City Planning Associates, Inc. 1969). The report maintained that nonwhite families and individuals occupied 52 percent of "deficient" housing units in the county despite comprising just about 4 percent of the county population (City Planning Associates,

2.3 Report cover, *Montgomery County Community Renewal Program Maryland R-39 (CR): Community Development Potential* (City Planning Associates, Inc. 1969).

Inc. 1969, 273). The recommendation given for Tobytown was the clearance of existing homes and the construction of "modern brick and wood" (Bonner 1974) public housing units in the neighborhood (see figure 2.4).

For Tobytown's urban renewal project, the Housing Authority of Montgomery County was awarded $775,082 in January 1972 by the US Department of Housing and Urban Development (HUD) (*Tribune* 1972). The plans called for the construction of twenty-six units that included nine duplexes and eight single-family townhouses. The plans also incorporated a recreational park and community center. Groundbreaking for the project took place in February 1972 (*Tribune* 1972), and the homes were completed in December 1972 (Bonner 1974), three months after Twyman's death.

Tobytown's urban renewal project was part of the national Turnkey III Homeownership Program for Low-Income Families. People living in public housing units under this program could acquire ownership of their homes by making income-based monthly payments that included a budgeted amount for maintenance and repair. A portion of these monthly payments was set aside in a reserve account credited toward residents' future

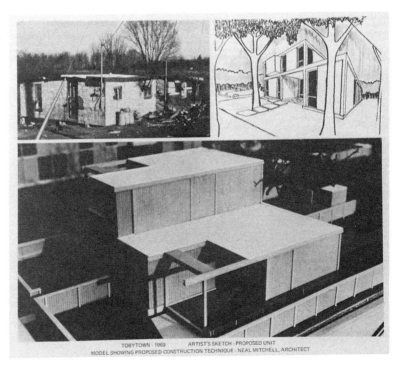

TOBYTOWN · 1969   ARTIST'S SKETCH - PROPOSED UNIT
MODEL SHOWING PROPOSED CONSTRUCTION TECHNIQUE - NEAL MITCHELL, ARCHITECT

2.4 Photograph of existing conditions and renderings of proposed construction for Tobytown's urban renewal project. *Top left*: Tobytown, 1969. *Top right*: Artist's sketch of a proposed housing unit. *Bottom*: Model of proposed construction (City Planning Associates, Inc. 1969, 173).

purchase of their homes. To qualify, applicants needed to meet certain standards of "potential for homeownership," including having sufficient income to make monthly payments and estimated monthly utility costs and having at least one resident family member with gainful employment or an established source of continuing income (US Government 1974). The program also stipulated terms and conditions that prohibited illicit activities and implicitly excluded single-parent woman-headed households and nontraditional family structures. The gender-exclusionary language specified that a homebuyer could not "use or occupy *his* home for any unlawful purpose" and must agree to use the home "only as a place to live for *himself* and *his* family (as identified in *his* initial application or by subsequent amendment with the approval of the Authority), for children thereafter born to or adopted by members of such family, and for aged or widowed parents of the Homebuyer or spouse who may join the household" (US

2.5 Photograph of Tobytown groundbreaking. Jane C. Sween Research Library and Special Collections, Montgomery History, Rockville, Maryland (Margaret Cudney Collection, Series IV: Subseries 1, Box 5).

Government 1974, emphasis added). Thus, the terms of qualification under Turnkey III—like those of other public housing programs—were particularly difficult, if not impossible, to meet for people living at the intersection of popular constructions of "deviance," including poor, Black, unmarried women; unemployed people; and people with disabilities (Rodriguez 2021).

The urban renewal project in Tobytown can be understood as a collective effort by county government officials and the federal government to put an end to the community's fugitive infrastructure. As a part of state-organized "slum clearance" efforts, urban renewal took place as a "spatial practice of . . . social control for individual Black deviance and collective community disorganization" (Rodriguez 2021, 58). Through this practice, poor and working-class Black communities were cast as concentrated sinks of crime and immorality that could be "fixed" spatially through development. This "spatial fix" (Harvey 2001) required Tobytown residents to sell and then buy back—on the government's terms—the land that their families had been living on for about one hundred years (see figure 2.6). While the Montgomery County Housing Opportunities Commission (HOC) paid out to residents just $29,800 for the fifteen acres of land on which the twenty-six new housing units and a park were built (Singh 1981), resi-

2.6 Photograph of an unnamed Tobytown resident signing a document related to the neighborhood's urban renewal project. Jane C. Sween Research Library and Special Collections, Montgomery History, Rockville, Maryland (Margaret Cudney Collection, Series IV: Subseries 1, Box 5).

dents had to pay for the homes, valued between $27,000 and $30,000 each (Wagner 1991). According to an article in the *Montgomery Journal*, "About 100 Tobytown residents moved into the 26 new units under the 'Home Buyers Association' plan with the contractual understanding that they were to rent the units with the option to buy" (Singh 1981). Their sustained ability to rent their homes, however, was contingent on behavior that was agreeable to county authorities.

In 1976, HOC officials formed a Blue Ribbon Committee to break a cycle characterized by what they termed a "clan psychology" of unemployment, intramarriage, and social degeneration in Tobytown (Wiener 1977). Such "culture of poverty" discourse echoed former assistant secretary of labor Daniel Patrick Moynihan's 1965 report on Black poverty in the United States, *The Negro Family: The Case for National Action*. Commonly known as the "Moynihan Report," this document naturalized crime as an outcome of "broken homes" headed by Black women in poor, urban neighborhoods. According to this logic, policing was increasingly rationalized as a legitimate and necessary answer to Black poverty, which was disconnected from the impacts of racial capitalism such as structural abandonment, austerity, and increasing concentrations of wealth (Loyd and Bonds 2018, 899). During Tobytown's urban renewal project, this took place as the Blue Ribbon Committee chose individuals and families from a list of tenants whom they believed should be evicted or asked to move based on nonpayment of rent, alcoholism, "refusal" to work, engaging in criminal activity, or overcrowding within a single unit. Through this committee, the right to housing in Tobytown was made conditional and increasingly restricted based on surveillance of residents and their past and imagined future crimes. In spring 1977, four of Tobytown's "most problem-prone families" were displaced, and, in their stead, the HOC sought out "models of upward mobility" who met the "strict criteria" of having "jobs, their own transportation, and stable family relationships" (Wiener 1977).

Beyond these evictions, attempts to police and eradicate Tobytown's fugitive infrastructure were largely unsuccessful. Whereas urban renewal programs identified spreading "crime and public disorder" as detrimental conditions of urban blight (President's Task Force on Urban Renewal 1970), Tobytown residents refused to reduce their community's fugitivity to a problem. Many residents were upset about having to rent from the county HOC and follow its terms of order. Several complained about the HOC's attacks on forms of community leisure and bonding activities and expressed dismay with the increased governance in Tobytown. For example, James Chambers noted disdainfully: "Nobody's causing problems here. We stand around, we drink sometimes, but we're not bothering anybody" (Wiener 1977). Likewise, Tobytown resident Lord Martin, who was about sixty years old at the time, complained about the changes. He explained that although the houses "back then" were falling apart, he liked his community much better: "I would much rather go back to living the way it was before. Then I could raise my hogs. Now I can't raise anything. They [officials] won't allow it" (Singh 1981). Many residents also worried about evictions and even refrained from sharing their experiences with news reporters due to fear of retaliation from the HOC (Singh 1981). Rufus Ragin, HOC tenant counsel, explained the discomfort that Tobytowners had with adjusting to the changes in their neighborhood: "It's like asking a fish to live on land" (Singh 1981). Put differently, as the *Washington Post* declared in a title for a 1982 article, "It Takes More Than a Facelift to Change Toby Town's Soul" (Walsh 1982) (figure 2.7). For Tobytown residents, their unboundedness from dominant terms of order played an important role in sustaining their livelihoods and sense of place.

2.7 "It Takes More Than a Facelift to Change Toby Town's Soul." From the *Washington Post*, July 7, 1982 (Walsh 1982). Photograph by Joseph McCary.

Nonconforming land uses constituted one example of fugitive infrastructure that survived urban renewal in Tobytown. For example, in 1974, only three residents had planted in the designated communal garden plot set aside during the previous year by the housing agency. Instead, residents like Henson Davis continued to use their existing gardens. After his home was replaced with an HOC-owned townhouse, Davis continued to maintain his backyard garden just some steps from his new back door, where he planted onion, cabbage, and tomato plants (Bonner 1974). Similarly, Tobytowner Lord Martin continued to "hunt rabbits and stuff" (Singh 1981). Perhaps seemingly insignificant, such responses by Tobytown residents to the urban renewal project in their neighborhood show how alternative relationships with land can take place within the constraints of state power and unfulfilled struggles for Black land.

Even Tobytowners' visions of land ownership underscore ongoing fugitivity as a bedrock of the community's infrastructure. For example, almost a decade after urban renewal in Tobytown, community resident Melvin Martin proclaimed: "Ain't no way I am going to give up my house. For this I will fight it out, even if it means going to jail. I am not going to rest until I own the house" (Singh 1981). Melvin Martin's proclamation speaks to what Andrea R. Roberts (2018, 68) calls "unkempt notions of . . . land ownership" through which "seemingly errant people or places" have been integral to historical Black communities and settlements across the United States. In the context of state-sanctioned racial dispossession, Black land and community can themselves be errant, or fugitive, acts. While Black land ownership that "appeals to the settler colonial state" should not be exempt from inter-rogation in ongoing structures of colonialism and capitalism (Pulido and De Lara 2018, 78), fugitive infrastructure is a framework for understanding Black land as capable of sustaining life outside registers of dispossession, domination, and profit.

Melvin Martin did eventually come to own his house. In 1982, he became the first Tobytown resident to purchase his HOC home after ten years of renting. It was not until another decade had passed after Martin purchased his home, however, that any other Tobytowners were able to purchase their homes. In the 1990s, four additional Tobytown residents became home-owners (Wagner 1991). A major factor in this delayed promise of home-ownership was that it took until 1981 for the county Housing Opportunities Commission to even create a procedure for Tobytown residents to buy their homes (Singh 1981). Prior to that, no purchase prices for the homes had been officially determined. Restructuring and increased surveillance of To-bytown was evidently more important than fulfilling the HOC's ostensible goal of homeownership for low-income families. By 1991, only fifty-five residents—a little more than half of the number of residents who origi-nally moved into the HOC housing units—were living in Tobytown (Wagner 1991). Washing over the history of displacement, HOC spokesperson Joyce Siegel celebrated that same year the fact that "very few" Tobytown residents have departed (Wagner 1991). Among Tobytowners who remained in the community, their experiences were fraught with decades of conflict with HOC employees about how the community should be run (Wraga 2003).

In December 2017, all remaining HOC housing units were sold to Toby-town residents. The community was then fully transferred from the stew-ardship of the HOC to the community's Homeowners' Association in 2018 (Housing Opportunities Commission of Montgomery County 2018). This transfer of power marked the end of a long battle for community control over housing in Tobytown that erupted with the policing of the neighbor-hood's residents and built environment in the 1970s.

Policing and Fugitive Infrastructure

The policing of Carolyn Twyman and the urban renewal project in her com-munity, Tobytown, can be understood as a linked effort by the local and federal government to ensure social, economic, and political stability in a predominately wealthy county via the extermination of fugitive infrastructure. Instead of improving livelihoods and homes in low-income, Black communities like Tobytown, urban renewal has functioned to constrain Black geographic possibilities and place Black people under increased surveillance. In this way, state and state-sanctioned development itself can be considered a form of policing. Even while operating beyond the borders of the criminal legal system, development programs like urban renewal intersect with practices of so-called community supervision such as parole and probation, and punishments like banishment from one's home. To give name to such "submerged, serpentine forms of punishment that work in legally hybrid and institutionally variegated ways," Katherine Beckett and Naomi Murakawa (2012, 222) use the phrase "shadow carceral state." They explain further that the shadow carceral state functions to expand "punitive power . . . through the blending of civil, administrative, and criminal legal authority" (222). Today, shadow carceral state geographies of development are still evident in government programs such as HUD's Promise Zones, created during the Barack Obama administration in 2013 to reduce crime while enhancing economic activity, private investment, educational outcomes, and public health in designated urban, rural, and tribal communities.

More directly, dominant processes of development customarily center police as prominent actors in "establishing order and paving the way for development" (Samara 2010, 199). For urban renewal and other large-scale public development projects, the use of police powers is foundational to the ability of the state to absorb private land and property (Rodriguez 2021). Police violence, like that enacted against Carolyn Twyman, is part and parcel of this geographic restructuring process. In threatening and ending the lives of particular groups of people, police reinforce the idea that certain people and the places that they come from are disposable and therefore ripe for violent visions of development. Further, any "lack of consensus" about the role of the state in such development schemes "requires greater coercion of some of that state's subjects" by the police (Gilmore and Gilmore 2016, 174).

At the same time, the unsuccessful conscriptions of local Black people into the spatial order of racial governance have enabled the maintenance of fugitive infrastructure brimming with radical possibility. In following in the footsteps of maroons, Twyman led a public rejection of policing rooted in a rupture in governance that had been put in place by people fleeing enslavement more than a century earlier. Likewise, Tobytown residents' negation of the constrictions of urban renewal in their community can be traced along a historical continuum of fugitivity. Their opposition to policing as a condition for investment in their neighborhood demonstrates how development can be imagined without policing. Together, the fugitivity of Carolyn Twyman and her fellow Tobytown residents model ways to live in and move through the world without police.

The fugitive infrastructure of Tobytown and other local Black communities speaks to a long tradition of marronage. For generations, over the course of more than two hundred years, residents of Black communities in Montgomery County have been fleeing and building community life outside the oppressions of state-making projects—including slavery, policing, and urban renewal. They remind us how "in the shadow of the real and fictive narrations of governmentality and the awesome powers of the state, there have always lurked individuals and communities embodying governing's unsuccessful inscriptions and conscriptions. Individuals and communities remain frequently unscripted and unimpressed by the state, even as they live under constant surveillance and suppression" (Quan 2017, 178). The work of Black people to construct and maintain fugitive infrastructure in the face of unremitting state and state-sanctioned violence is both a painful indictment of and a radical departure from the racial capitalist state's terms of order.

As evidenced by the long historical arc connecting the troop of maroons with Carolyn Twyman and her community of Tobytown, fugitivity is an actively evolving practice that enables Black residents to respond to shifting structural conditions and the police violence mobilized to facilitate those transformations. Marronage, then, is not simply a metaphor by which to describe the endurance of Black fugitivity in postslavery contexts. Metaphors "delinked from their material underpinnings or histories" risk casting racial violence and Black flight as "figurative" rather than concrete and embodied (McKittrick 2021, 11). In contrast, locating Black flight from and placemaking beyond policing within maroon geographies underscores the tangibility and applicability of often abstracted imaginaries for police abolition. Residents' challenges and interruptions of local attempts at governance point toward a history and a future of local Black abolitionist praxes rooted in marronage. In the next chapter, I discuss some alternatives to criminal punishment shaping maroon geographies in Montgomery County.

From their initial development, maroon geographies have required definitions and systems of justice beyond state-based criminal legal institutions. The act of marronage in itself was a form of breaking the law, with fugitives from slavery "stealing" away their bodies and labor from the confines of slavery. Moreover, once on the path toward freedom, maroons needed to evade police and state-sanctioned authorities (often tasked with catching runaways) and define safety and security for themselves beyond policing. Any reliance on police would mean calling for their own re-enslavement. Likewise, for free Black people, establishing methods for dealing with issues outside of official authorities was necessary because they could be enslaved if convicted of a crime. The need for alternative forms of safety and security beyond policing thus shaped early maroon geographies and allowed Black people to circumvent further subjecting themselves and their communities to the violence of slavery. In Black communities in Montgomery County, after slavery was abolished, an ethic of marronage continued to shape how residents resolved conflicts and repaired relationships after disputes. In this chapter, I discuss how "maroon justice" takes place in historically Black communities in Montgomery County. Key principles of maroon justice are community-based accountability, the rejection of value systems that hierarchically categorize people when harms occur, and structural solutions to conflict and violence. These principles have facilitated Black survival and independence in the wake of a dominant criminal legal system that underwrites Black death and suffering.

Maroon justice lies within the constellation of practices known as restorative and transformative justice. Restorative justice, which encompasses coordinated efforts by groups of people to collectively repair relationships and restore peace following conflicts and violence, "has been the dominant model of criminal justice throughout most of human history for perhaps all the world's people" (Braithwaite 2002, 5). Restorative justice existed before modern criminal legal systems and continues to operate alongside and beyond these systems. In the colonial Americas, maroon justice developed as enslaved and free Black people synthesized dispute resolution techniques rooted in African customs and rituals that centered community and cooperation rather than individualism and punishment (Jenkins 2006). Interlinked with restorative justice, transformative justice gives name to efforts by people to achieve broader collective liberation alongside restoring individual and community well-being (Kershnar et al. 2007). Transformative justice is "a liberatory approach to violence . . . [that] seeks safety and accountability without relying on alienation, punishment, or State and systemic violence, including incarceration and policing . . . [And it aims to transform the] conditions that allow violence to occur" (Kershnar et al. 2007, 5). Like restorative justice practices, approaches to transformative justice have shaped Black, Indigenous, and other marginalized communities across generations in their efforts to create safety and respond to interpersonal harm and harmful structural conditions (Mingus 2019).

In its restorative and transformative functions, maroon justice is a model for keeping communities intact rather than splintering them through policing and incarceration. Whereas the formal US criminal legal system is centered on punishment and removal—arresting people suspected of wrongdoing, doling out sentences to people convicted of crimes, isolating them from their communities, and locking them behind bars—maroon justice serves to maintain freedom and community. For generations, maroon justice in Montgomery County has enabled Black residents to heal from harm, hold one another accountable, and maintain safe communities.

Community-Based Accountability

The development of community-based systems of accountability is a cornerstone of maroon justice. Such systems empower communities to identify harm, attend to people who have been harmed, create measures for people to take responsibility for harms they have done, and prevent violence without reliance on the state and its agents of authority. Community-based accountability functions through a collective rather than individualistic approach toward safety and security. Such collectivism is what makes it possible for people to turn toward one another rather than turning toward police when issues arise. As the US-based national activist organization

INCITE! (2003) posits: "If we ask the question, What can I do?, then the only answer will be to call the police. If we ask the question, what can we do? then we may be surprised at the number of strategies we can devise."

In Montgomery County's Black communities, community-based accountability has been practiced and maintained through close-knit relationships between residents and by strong community institutions. Residents across the history of local Black communities describe environments in which neighbors look out for one another. Residents also established networks of people tasked with responding to issues in their communities. In the community of Haiti, for example, local men were called on as the first line of response when issues arose. Moreover, in many communities, extended family members often lived in such close proximity to one another that they could be called to resolve domestic disputes. For example, in interviews with residents of the historically Black Sandy Spring area, I was told that police were never called to respond to frequent domestic disputes in the community. Instead, relatives were called, and they would settle any disputes. These maroon justice practices move away from the state as the primary arbitrator for addressing issues and instead center community relationships.

Alongside these everyday relationships, Black churches are central to community-based accountability in maroon justice. Throughout the United States, the Black church developed as "a multifaceted religious, social, economic, educational, cultural, political institution with a broad range of social structures and social functions" that addressed the needs of Black communities following emancipation (Billingsley 2003, 9). As part of this range of functions, Black churches established informal justice procedures to arbitrate disputes and harms within their communities. The origins of Black church-based justice practices can be traced to African cultural techniques for social control and dispute resolution passed down generationally by enslaved Black people and their descendants. In the Gullah Islands of South Carolina, for example, praise houses practiced community-based grievance processes rooted in West African customs such as requiring a community member who stole from another to pick up a *benne* (sesame) seed with their nose in order to restore their place in the community (Jenkins 2006). Throughout the first half of the twentieth century, leaders of praise houses in the Gullah community handled disputes through requiring rituals like this, spiritually based counseling for those who violated community norms, and/or material or nonmaterial reparations for the harmed person(s). Very few disputes were taken to outside authorities, and community members who did so were often scorned and banished from the island (Jenkins 2006).[1]

Similar to the centrality of praise houses in Gullah justice practices, Black churches in Montgomery County were known for expressing "the highest moral codes of the community and standards for what one 'ought' to do and believe" (McDaniel 1979a, 31). When the Black community of Sugarland was a thriving neighborhood, community-based accountability was ensured through a justice system at the community church (figure 3.1). Built in 1871, Sugarland church was the focal point of the neighborhood. The church served numerous roles, from operating as a school prior to the racial integration of the local public school system to acting as a community center. Sugarland church also served as a space of community-based governance and operated as a courthouse for Sugarland residents. Describing this function of the church, former Sugarland resident Gwendora Hebron Reese explained that residents "set up their own rules and regulations. When they had problems, they brought it before the church and the pastor would act as the judge and they would appoint others to defend and that sort of thing, and they held the sessions right here in the church" (*Community Cornerstones* 2014). In this way, disputes between community members were settled by church members and church leadership. Cases, some of which are detailed in the church's old register (figure 3.2), ranged from family disputes to church matters.

In October 1885, for example, a forty-eight-year-old man named John Higgins was found guilty of taking a fifteen-year-old girl into his family's home after her grandmother told her to "take your dirty rags you stinking huzzie and go away from here." While the full details of this case are unclear, the example of a man taking in a girl too young to offer consent invites consideration of the possibilities of community-based accountability systems for sexual violence. As an alternative to state institutions proven to "deepen the harm caused by household and community violence" (Richie 2012, 139), the Sugarland church provided a safe space for community members to call into question the intimate relationship and age difference between the man and the girl. Higgins was then held accountable for his actions beyond the violence of the state. His punishment was ex-communication from the church for a temporary time period, a frequent punishment meted out following a guilty verdict in Sugarland. This allowed people who caused harm or violated shared standards to remain in the community at large, while

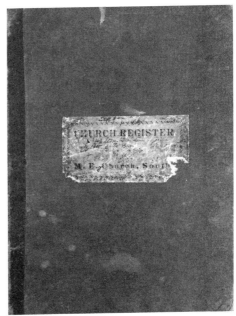

3.1 *(left)* Sugarland church around 1900. Photograph provided by Sugarland Ethno-History Project.

3.2 *(right)* Sugarland church register. Photograph by author.

reducing contact with affected community members until relationship repairs could be attempted.

In addition to the justice procedures themselves, the use of the church register to record community conflict proceedings is representative of Sugarland's approach to justice. In the register, descriptions of cases about disputes are inscribed between pages filled with other church business, including lists of church member names, death registries, and details about the reconstruction of the church in 1893 after the original structure was destroyed by a fire. When read as part of a consecutive narrative, the cases in Sugarland's church register exemplify the everyday business of conflict management and community accountability. Rather than relying on the extraordinary use of force by the state, Sugarland residents mobilized ordinary community resources and institutions to practice justice. Moreover, the text in the register differs sharply from criminal records that permanently mark people as deviant and valueless. The register allows one to take into view the broader lives and contributions of people who have enacted harm against others. For example, the same year that he was found guilty of taking a young girl into his home, John Higgins helped bring to the church's attention a case of a Sugarland schoolteacher whom he claimed was not serving the best interests of his students. In this way, the Sugarland church register situates acts that may be otherwise deemed criminal within an understanding of that person's expansive and valuable life.

Sugarland's method of community conflict mediation is attributed by former residents to the efforts of early residents to counteract the violence of slavery. As Reese explained: "The families . . . wanted to build a community that was in opposition to slavery" (*Community Cornerstones* 2014). Multigenerational practices like the use of the church as a courthouse were developed in Sugarland in order to isolate the community from the larger society and to ensure that Black families were not dislocated like they so easily were during slavery. In an interview with me, Reese further elucidated that early residents "knew all of the pitfalls of slavery when they were enslaved. They knew about how the families were torn apart, that sort of thing. So, when they formed the community, they wanted to make sure that that bond was there so that you didn't have to worry about somebody coming in and taking this person and that person." Those practices were then passed down to subsequent generations of Sugarland residents. Maroon justice remained an integral part of Black flight after slavery's end by helping residents evade capture and violence by the state.

Similar community-based accountability systems shaped conflict resolution practices in Ken-Gar and Lincoln Park. Black residents often rejected policing as a condition for the maintenance of peace in their communities. A leader of the Ken-Gar community named Leonard Jackson—also known as the unofficial "mayor" of Ken-Gar—often patrolled the streets of the neighborhood. If he saw something out of character, he would call around to other residents, who would, in turn, call their neighbors to deal with issues in the community. As one former Ken-Gar resident shared with me, by the time the call got to you, "if you didn't say anything, you were questioned." In Lincoln Park during the 1980s, residents developed a phone system similar to that in Ken-Gar that enabled residents to discuss and respond to incidents in the community without relying on police as first responders. A resident of Lincoln Park who has lived in the community for seven decades explained how the phone line operated: "We had people on every street. If you saw anything, you were to call one person, and this one person will contact the police so that everybody wouldn't be callin' the police." The police were seldom called; in interviews with Lincoln Park residents, I was told that the phone line resulted in the police being called only "once or twice." The phone line mainly allowed community members to get "on the same page," to stay aware of "what was going on in the neighborhood" and, at times, to "squash rumors." Calling one another in this manner before calling police provided opportunities for Lincoln Park and Ken-Gar residents to repair issues in their communities on their own terms, and to protect themselves from the violence of police intervention.

Community-based accountability systems were put in place for children as well. Rather than individualizing the care and discipline of youth, Black community residents collectively watched after them. When the children got into mischief, any adult community member could discipline them, and the news of their behavior quickly spread. As former Sugarland resident Billy Lyle recalled:

> Them old folks did not play. They made us go into the woods and pick out our switch—and not just any switch, it had to be the right flexibility (springy), and if it was not right, you had to march back into the woods and get another one. What made it so bad was that no matter whose house you were at, they had the right to measure out discipline to you as they would to their own children, the way they saw fit. When you arrived home, the look on your parents' face let you know you were in for another trip to the woods for another switch. They would usually wait until you were changing for bed and come in switch in hand. It was not so much to hurt you physically, but to sting your bottom and give you something to think about. (R. Davis 2015)

In addition to homes in the neighborhood, community institutions served as spaces for neighborhood youth to resolve their issues and to learn community-based accountability measures. A prime illustration of youth-focused accountability systems was a sign posted in 1990 in the Lincoln Park Recreation Center at children's eye level reminding local youth that "teasing, tattle-telling, and cussing" were not allowed at the center. The sign warned that a twenty-five-cent fine would be charged for each offense (Gregg 1990). In this way, children were held responsible for their behavior and were encouraged to work out everyday issues rather than escalate disputes to adult authority figures. Such measures set the ground for children to understand their peer community as a space for conflict resolution and accountability.

The lesson emergent from community-based accountability in local Black communities is the significance of care. For generations, residents have practiced "care laterally . . . in a different relation than that of the violence of the state" (Sharpe 2016, 20). This is not to say that violence and other typical criminal punishment techniques did not occur within Black communities' systems of accountability. Tools of discipline such as switches and ostracism brought corporal punishment and social exclusion into broader maroon justice practices. Additionally, the central role of the Black church meant that maroon justice was often couched in religious sexual mores that, while helping protect young people who could not consent to sex, also contributed to the discrimination of community members who practiced nonmonogamy, were openly gay or lesbian, or otherwise challenged beliefs about sexuality passed on to Black churches from white Christianity (Frazier 1974; Griffin 2000). While the archival record on Montgomery County's historically Black communities bears little to no mention of queer sexuality to my knowledge, this absence implicitly marks heterosexuality as the solely legitimate and standard sexuality. In spite of these limits of maroon justice, Black community members have defined and practiced their own forms of community accountability that transcend rather than reproduce the procedural violence of the US criminal legal system. They model ways to hold community members accountable for their actions without incarceration and related lifelong consequences such as job insecurity and disenfranchisement.

Rejecting Dominant Ideas of Criminality

Part of what has enabled local Black communities to maintain community-based systems of accountability is their rejection of value systems that sort people according to their supposed guilt or innocence. Again, because the practice of marronage itself was a form of breaking the law, maroon geographies have always necessitated such a rejection. Marronage was predicated upon the refusal of Black people to accept the legal constriction of their physical and social mobility. The rejection of dominant notions of legality and illegality has, therefore, long been a basis of radical Black political praxis.

A key example of this refutation comes from Ken-Gar, where residents mobilized against police involvement and the arrest and incarceration of community members linked to a killing and assault in 1972. On the night of Friday, August 18, 1972, a group of three white teenagers drove into Ken-

Gar and threw firecrackers into a group of community residents. Some Ken-Gar residents responded by shooting and killing the driver of the car and beating one of the passengers. The other passenger ran away. When the Montgomery County police attempted to begin their investigation of the incident and make arrests, community leader Leonard Jackson was able to convince the police to not enter the neighborhood. He was concerned that police intervention would incite further unrest. In exchange for their non-involvement, Jackson patrolled the streets of Ken-Gar that night and the following night. Police maintained their end of the moratorium agreement until 5:00 a.m. on Sunday morning, "when Jackson was notified by angry neighbors that a team of shotgun-wielding police with dogs had descended on the neighborhood" (Magruder 1976). Many Ken-Gar residents critiqued the intrusion by police officers and condemned the subsequent police searches as "unnecessarily brusque" (Magruder 1976).

While brief, the space of freedom afforded by delayed police involvement allowed residents to protect themselves from the chaos that an immediate law enforcement response would have likely brought. For example, a Ken-Gar resident who was nine years old at the time of the incident remembers being able to go to sleep that night without the knowledge that anything serious had occurred. In an interview with me, he described his experience that night: "I was walking through Ken-Gar . . . and I heard all of the noise, the firecrackers and everything going off. I never thought anything about it until the next day everything was brought to light about what had happened."

In addition, even after police involvement, residents worked together to prevent the incarceration of the Ken-Gar residents who were connected to the incident. When five Ken-Gar men—referred to as the Ken-Gar 5—were detained and charged with murder, assault, and/or battery, residents were able to pool together bond money for four of the five men. When one of the Ken-Gar 5, twenty-eight-year-old Gene P. Hopkins, was found guilty of manslaughter and sentenced to ten years in prison, the Ken-Gar community rallied together and petitioned for his release (Simpson 2013). He was released on parole less than four years later in February 1976 and returned to Ken-Gar.

Remarkably, Ken-Gar residents' mobilization against the incarceration of Hopkins did not center on an argument for his innocence, though it easily could have. Residents believed that Hopkins surrendered himself in place of a younger family member. Instead of maintaining Hopkins's innocence, however, Ken-Gar residents acknowledged the harms enacted against the white youth in an effort to facilitate healing. They issued a statement expressing regret for the death and injuries resulting from the confrontation between Ken-Gar residents and the white teenagers (Simpson 2013).

The rejection of innocence as a precondition for Ken-Gar's mobilizations against policing and incarceration is a critical argument for police abolition. Ken-Gar residents' approach toward seeking justice after the 1972 murder rested on their knowledge of the structural conditions of anti-Blackness. They understood residents' confrontation with the white teenagers as a response to a long history of racial violence to which their community had been subjected. In addition to the firecracker incident, the neighborhood was plagued by a violent pattern of harassment and assaults. Residents had dealt with Ku Klux Klan intimidation, had been beaten in their own yards by white youth, and had experienced gunshots being fired into the community from across the railroad tracks that form one of its borders (*Washington Area Spark* 1972c). In the aftermath of the Ken-Gar 5's arrests, the *Washington Area Spark* (1972a) reported that white youth were known to drive to Ken-Gar and shout racial epithets at residents up to four times a week; while the white teenagers' firecracker attack was minimized as another "prank," the Ken-Gar 5 faced long-term incarceration (figure 3.3). Accordingly, Ken-Gar residents saw police intervention in their community as part of a system that has routinely sanctioned and contributed to such violence by defending whiteness and criminalizing Blackness. Building from this epistemology of racial violence, Ken-Gar residents refused to formulate their defense of the Ken-Gar 5 around the reasoning of the US criminal legal system. Their struggle for justice centered on alternative measures to account for and redress harm regardless of any official determination of guilt or innocence.

Ken-Gar residents' efforts to free the Ken-Gar 5 demonstrate that challenges against policing and incarceration are not best won by arguing that innocent people have been wrongly convicted. If challenges to the criminal legal system only constitute moments when people point out "innocents among the convicted or killed" (Gilmore 2017, 234), the system is upheld rather than unraveled. As Gilmore argues, "for abolition, to insist on innocence is to surrender politically because 'innocence' evades a problem abolition is compelled to confront: how to diminish and remedy harm as against finding better forms of punishment" (2017, 236). In other words, effective challenges to policing must demand more than a perfect operationalization of the US criminal legal system's central logic: the suspicion and

5 Ken-Gar residents arrested for murder after racists attack their community

Ken-Gar, slumlord-owned black section of Kensington, has long been a favorite place for white kids to vent their racist hate. They like to drive through the area, especially on Plyers Mill Road, shouting nigger and other epithets at the people who live there. This happens about four times a week.

About two weeks ago, three Wheaton men, one of whom was about to go into the Marines, went riding down Plyers Mill throwing firecrackers out of their car window at the people on the street. Plyers Mill dead-ends in Ken-Gar, and they were about to turn the car around when they were approached by several of the neighborhood people. One of the whites got away, but one of the other two was beaten up and the Marine recruit was fatally shot. Five people are charged with murder.

Mark Murray, 18, the dead white man, obviously cannot pay more for his crime. A 17-year-old Wheaton man got injured, but nobody knows who he is. And Arthur Lineberry, of 12904 Neola Road, Silver Spring, 949-8236, ran away. Because of their prank, as their parents and friends call it, five men face long imprisonment and ruined lives.

Four of the five men charged with murder have been released. Gordon Hall and Richard Dorsey were released on 1,000 personal bond; John Kaine was released on two 500 bonds, one for murder and one for assault with intent to murder; and Gene Hopkins was released on 5,000 bond. David Kelly, at the time of this writing, is still in the Montgomery jail on 2,000 bond. A preliminary hearing has been set for September 11.

The people of Ken-Gar continue to be harrassed. They continue to receive threatening phone calls from disgruntled white racists; a hearse with the word DEATH painted on the side was driven through the community three days after the incident; and a shot was fired into the community four days after the incident. Shots have been fired into the neighborhood many times before, just to harrass the people.

Black people in America have had a long history of fighting back against racism and oppression. It is clear that the residents of Ken-Gar are fed up with racist attacks. Decent citizens both black and white need to rally behind the five young men indicted for the defense of their community. If you are interested in putting something together, contact the Spark office at Montgomery College in Rockville.

3.3 Newspaper article about the Ken-Gar 5. From the *Washington Area Spark*, September 6, 1972.

later determination of a suspect's guilt as justification for one's arrest, incarceration, and lifetime label of "criminal." Even in the event that every person swept up by police and locked away in jails and prisons is "rightfully" convicted, abolition requires dismantling the criminal legal system and building something new and different. It requires disavowing the legal confines that make anyone deemed fit for captivity or premature death in the first place.

Across Montgomery County, Black community members habitually exhibited this abolitionist praxis by eschewing state notions of criminality. Multiple residents of local Black communities, for example, informed me of incidents they witnessed in which they could have called the police but chose not to. A resident of Lincoln Park who has lived in the community for seven decades recalled calling the police only on two occasions. For the most part, she has steered clear of intervening in matters. She explained,

> I've seen stuff that I could've easily called [the police for]. But I didn't. . . . Sometimes, you know, it's not worth it, because you don't want to be sitting up in court being no witness against nobody. . . . No, I have bigger battles to fight. Yeah, you learn how to step back. You know, you just can't go out there and tackle everything. You have to pick your battles. . . . So I've seen a lot of stuff over the years. Nothing that's ever made me afraid to lock my doors or want to move, but I've seen stuff. Yeah, but I didn't tell it.

For many residents of Montgomery County's historically Black communities, calling the police was mostly a last resort, something that they rarely or never did during their lifetimes. An eighty-three-year-old lifelong resident of Scotland summed up the majority of local Black residents' experiences when he told me that he has "never called the police for anything." At the heart of residents' refusal to rely on the police is a radical understanding of human value and conflict resolution beyond the state's anti-Black delineation of guilt and innocence. This refusal of policing has allowed local Black residents to develop community-based structural solutions to harm instead of relying mainly on the criminal legal system.

Structural Solutions to Harm

Undergirding maroon justice across Montgomery County's historically Black communities is a structural approach to interpersonal violence and other behaviors deemed harmful by residents. Rather than routinely criminalizing and seeking out punishment for individuals who enact harms against themselves and others or who otherwise threaten established social norms, residents have fostered community-based strategies that disrupt the structural forces that lead to harm. This structural approach is based in a crucial acknowledgment that "incarceration and prison-backed policing neither redress nor repair the very sorts of harms they are supposed to address—interpersonal violence, addiction, mental illness, and sexual abuse, among others" (McLeod 2015, 1156). Instead, what local Black residents have demonstrated for generations is that harms are best addressed and prevented through investments in human needs.

In Tobytown during the 1960s, for example, residents worked together to combat harmful behaviors by demanding investments in neighborhood improvements and organizing education and employment initiatives. During that time, issues such as gambling, alcohol abuse, and poor living conditions were often the focus of news about Tobytown. County officials and white residents largely considered Tobytown a "bad" place with "bad" people. Arthur B. Hayes III, a Tobytown resident, expressed dismay at this reputation and at the solutions proposed for Tobytown by outsiders:

> Now much has been said of Tobytown, in Montgomery County and beyond it, it has gained a reputation that has generated a degree of fear. . . . The basis of fear is ignorance. Almost everyone is ignorant of Tobytown. Par-

ticularly ignorant are those who go there out of curiosity and then feel they have become authorities on the community, its problems, structure and pat solutions. I have read that stricter gambling laws, less drinking and church attendance will meet the basic requirements for the problems that Tobytown faces. I have heard the people of Tobytown called beasts and the solution offered, that the men ought to be locked up, the women sent to camps, the children put up for adoption and the place bulldozed. What manner of men are those who would speak so? . . . It would seem that some would use the approach to social problems that Adolf Hitler found so effective in dealing with troublesome minorities. ("Montgomery County Commission on Human Relations Minutes" 1965)

In contrast to the violent approach suggested by outsiders to combat issues in Tobytown, community members developed their own structural solutions. Tobytowners organized and participated in a series of community meetings and made collective decisions about the future of their community. Structural solutions that emerged as a product of these meetings included the provision of a trash can for every home and the construction of outhouses. Further solutions were Tobytown women's participation in home budgeting and food buying extension courses at the University of Maryland, and the seeking out of year-round employment by neighborhood men. Residents were also able to promote literacy in their community through a partnership with the Literacy Council of Montgomery County, Maryland, a nonprofit organization founded in 1963. Additionally, during the 1970s, Reverend Howard Scales of the Tobytown church began holding church services on Saturday nights in order to help combat gambling—which used to take place primarily on Saturday nights. He even baptized the leader of the community gambling ring (Bonner 1974). Almost one hundred years following the case of John Higgins in Sugarland described earlier, the Black church—along with sanitation infrastructure, education, and economic investment—remained a site of community-based solutions to structurally criminalized activities.

These people-centered solutions model how resources may be shifted away from policing to support community organizing, social services, and infrastructural improvements. The point here is not that missing trash cans, absent public restrooms, separation from religion, or nonheteronormative, non-middle-class gender roles lead to crime. Rather, such false notions strongly shape dominant treatments of crime such as the 1965 Moynihan report—which linked urban crime to the declining Black nuclear family—and later, James Q. Wilson and George L. Kelling's broken windows theory (1982), which promoted the idea that visible signs of "civil disorder" like litter and public urination lead to increased rates of crime and therefore should be targeted by police. In a context where policing and surveillance in Black communities were increasingly justified based on such notions of disorder, Tobytown residents' struggles for investments in community infrastructure, family education, employment, and religious institutions can be understood as efforts to transform the conditions with which crime was associated and policing was justified.

Across Black communities in Montgomery County, structural solutions to harm have been mobilized as an alternative to reliance on criminal law. Black residents have worked together to secure state investment in their communities, develop educational programs, secure stable employment opportunities, and more. These structural solutions to harm are based in a local, multigenerational practice of reimagining community safety and security through the lens of human needs. Situating human needs as the focus of harm redress and prevention allows us to ask how we can help all of us rather than some of us—a question that demands an answer beyond the individualized response of criminal law enforcement. Chapter 4 will return to local visions of community-centered infrastructures as alternatives to police.

Contradictions of Maroon Justice

The notion of maroon justice offers a useful framework for understanding multigenerational alternatives to policing that shape maroon geographies. It is important to emphasize, however, that the principles of maroon justice are not unconscious ideals that automatically reproduce themselves in the space of relatively autonomous Black communities. Rather, maroon justice comprises a set of practices that are continuously reinforced and at times also contradicted. Over time, various historical conditions and societal pressures have prompted residents of Montgomery County's maroon geographies to sometimes shift away from the principles of maroon justice and toward traditional policing mechanisms. In particular, increasing drug use and sales during the 1970s through the 1990s in local Black communities caused many residents to support increased police involvement in their neighborhoods. In the midst of a national "war on drugs"—an initiative and set of policies put in place by the US government beginning in the 1970s—some residents embraced harsher penalties and increased law enforcement as solutions to drug activity in their neighborhoods. The war on drugs was a major inflection point in Black communities, lessening the distance between themselves and the violence of the state.

During the 1970s and 1980s, for example, residents of the Scotland community grappled with the tensions of adhering to community-based justice practices and taking advantage of legal systems put in place by the state. These tensions followed on the heels of a HUD-funded urban renewal project completed in Scotland in 1971. While Scotland residents had an established reputation of independently functioning without much involvement from local government agencies, an increasing problem with drug activity sparked conflicting approaches to safety, security, and justice in the community ("Memorandum" 1975). After a series of drug-related shootings and assaults committed by a family in their community in 1975, for instance, some Scotland residents resisted involving the police. After someone was killed, a resident whom people believed knew relevant details about the killing would not volunteer the information. Other residents of Scotland cooperated with police investigations, sharing suspect names and waiting for the police investigation to be completed before taking any action themselves. At the same time, the residents who cooperated with the police investigation also exhibited a willingness to handle matters themselves through extralegal conflict resolution. A 1975 memorandum on "unrest in the Scotland community" expressed this readiness: "The Scotland Community has had enough . . . and will take their own action if the family [committing the violence] is not forced to leave the community." The family members involved in the shootings and assaults were eventually evicted from their homes in Scotland. There was no mention in the archives of any arrests or incarceration surrounding the incidents.

Following this, Scotland residents began participating in measures such as the State of Maryland Families Insisting on Safe Tenancies (FIST) program to combat drug activity in their neighborhood (Phibbs 1990). The FIST program was created in 1989 by the Maryland Department of Housing and Community Development to facilitate the process of evicting tenants found guilty of drug violations, including manufacturing, selling, distributing, dispensing, or storing drugs, on or near the premises of their rented homes. Landlords and rental management personnel registered for the FIST program were supplied with arrest information from police departments regarding drug-related arrests on their properties. They were then able to immediately evict tenants involved in drug activity. In addition to their cooperation with the FIST program, Scotland residents were celebrated by the Montgomery County police for their "willingness to help" in the provision of information about criminal activities (Phibbs 1990). When I visited Scotland in 2018, the Scotland Community Office still bore evidence of the FIST program: a yellow sign declaring that it is a FIST property and warning drug traffickers to "beware" (figure 3.4). The sign, however, appeared as more of a remnant of past policing than an indication of a continued antidrug program with the names of former Maryland governor Parris N. Glendening (1995–2003) and former Montgomery County executive Douglas M. Duncan (1994–2006) printed at the bottom of the sign.

While participating in these programs of state governance, Scotland residents also expanded their own internal capacity to respond to and prevent drug activity, violence, and conflict in their neighborhood. In 1986, Scotland residents organized a leadership program that held monthly workshops on topics such as problem solving, conflict management, and community involvement (Phibbs 1990). Scotland residents also organized other efforts, such as the Scotland Community Action Team (SCAT!), a group of "concerned adults" who met monthly to discuss issues like alcohol and drug abuse prevention, adequate child care and supervision, the need for nighttime activities for adults, the maintenance of a tutoring program, and overall community health and happiness ("SCAT!," n.d.).[2] Another community-based effort was the Scotland Mentoring Program—a partnership between the Scotland Community Civic Association, the Montgomery County Recreation Department, the Task Force on Mentoring of Montgomery County, and the Maryland Humanities Council—which was started as a response to a fight involving Scotland youth at a local high school in January 2007 (Donaghue 2008). These community-based efforts embody the principles of maroon justice, with community members determining for themselves how safety measures should take form and how to recover from and prevent conflict and violence.

Similar to Scotland residents, Lincoln Park community members struggled with how to respond to drug activity in their neighborhood during the 1980s and 1990s. When the Rockville and Montgomery County police departments began special patrols of Lincoln Park in 1988 and installed a police substation in the community in 1990 as a response to local drug sales and usage, some residents embraced this increased policing and others rejected it. Among those who accepted the increased involvement of police in Lincoln Park were members of the East Rockville Community Action Team,

3.4 State of Maryland Families Insisting on Safe Tenancies (FIST) program sign on the Scotland Community Center, 2018. Photograph by author.

organized in 1987. The community action team held weekly meetings to discuss neighborhood issues. Beginning in 1990, members also led marches on Friday nights during which they would walk the streets of the neighborhood while escorted by Rockville City and Montgomery County police officers. The marches, which variously numbered between ten people and more than forty, were intended to curtail drug activity in Lincoln Park on Friday nights and to send a message that the streets of Lincoln Park should be drug free. One of the ways that other Lincoln Park residents expressed their rejection of increased policing in their neighborhood was publicly denouncing the activities of the East Rockville Community Action Team. In fact, some Lincoln Park residents would stand on the sidelines and heckle Community Action Team members as they walked by (Nurmi 1990).

While the East Rockville Community Action Team worked in collaboration with police officers, the group did not patrol the neighborhood following the traditional logics of policing. According to an interview with one of the former members of the East Rockville Community Action Team, the marches worked by altering the geography of drug sales in the community rather than facilitating the arrests of people using and selling drugs. She explained that when the marchers would approach people selling drugs on the street, they would walk away: "They might come back after we left, but they would always move. Yeah, so they were constantly moving. They'd move from one street to the next, and when we'd get to that, then we were moving them again. But they didn't have time to make their sales if they were constantly moving. That was the main goal, and that's what happened." The former East Rockville Community Action Team member also explained that there were never any confrontations between marchers and people selling drugs. The action team's Friday night marches worked by stimulating mobility versus supporting arrests and confinement. This politics of mobility, which can be thought of as a vestige of the local history of marronage, was successful. During the marches, drug activity was significantly curtailed. In fact, people known for dealing and using drugs in the neighborhood would often join the marches—sometimes out of curiosity and also likely because they had friends and family whom they wanted to walk with. The action team members welcomed their participation, happy that it prevented them from using or selling drugs for at least the duration of the march (Nurmi 1990). The East Rockville Community Action Team operated throughout the early 1990s. This form of community cooperation with police is still evident today in the attendance of the Lincoln Park Civic Association's monthly meetings by Rockville police officers, who share city-wide crime statistics and safety-related recommendations with residents (Lincoln Park Civic Association, n.d.).

More generally, residents across Montgomery County's Black communities have also called for police involvement when faced with issues more mundane than drug activity and violence. For example, one Lincoln Park resident describes the chief of police as her "go-to person" to call when she notices issues in Lincoln Park. Over the years, however, she has mainly called the police to request them to have cars ticketed when parked at the end of her driveway and she is unable to reach the vehicle owner. Only one time could she recall ever contacting the police for a matter of safety. In that instance, she thought she had heard someone in her backyard and, because she was home alone that night, she called the police and had them search the perimeter of her property.

Some Black residents even established official ties with local police. As early as the 1890s, Haiti resident George Meads was appointed by the Montgomery County sheriff to serve as one of several deputy sheriffs tasked with pursuing people suspected of crimes and making arrests. During his tenure as the sole Black deputy sheriff until he died in 1919, Meads helped combat illegal liquor sales in 1899 and thwart a jail break in 1903

(Hedlund 2022). Meads is also credited with helping prove the innocence of a Haiti man named Tocha Martin, who was jailed around 1910 after being falsely accused of raping a white girl (Hedlund 2022). George Meads's son, Jesse Meads, was appointed deputy sheriff after his father's death and continued to serve throughout the 1920s. Decades later in Ken-Gar, the community leader Leonard Jackson who was known for turning away the police—most notably after that flare-up of racial tensions on a summer night in 1972—volunteered for police training. Jackson participated in the Montgomery County Police Citizen Academy in 1995 (figure 3.5). The Citizen Academy, which is a series of classes about policing, was created in 1994 as a way to increase county residents' awareness and support of the functions of the Montgomery County Police Department.

These examples of contradiction provide lessons for how to grapple with a project of abolition when the path to ending policing is not clear-cut. They demonstrate how people are sometimes compelled to embrace police as part of struggles for investments in safety and security for their communities. The contradictions of maroon justice also highlight how temporary negotiations and strategic cooperation with police can help uphold a long-term investment in the cultivation of places relatively free of police involvement. In Scotland, for example, cooperation with police was part of a larger community-based effort to expand internal capacity to respond to and prevent drug activity. Local Black communities' collaborations with police also suggest ways to rework the logics and resources of policing like in Lincoln Park, where residents took advantage of police presence in their neighborhood to combat drug activity on their own terms—without violent confrontations and arrests. Limited options for state investments in safety and security can be stretched to accomplish strategic goals toward abolition.

Compromises along the path toward abolition are, in fact, another legacy of marronage—a liminal state between bondage and the complete abolition of slavery in which freedom was often fleeting. At times, maroons had to leave behind or turn in other freedom seekers in exchange for their own freedom. Even some of the most formidable maroon settlements in Jamaica and Suriname, for example, compromised with state authorities by turning over runaways in exchange for official recognition of their independence (Diouf 2014, 307). Moreover, a majority of those left behind by maroons were enslaved children and the women who bore and raised them. While women did contribute to marronage by harboring and caring for maroons and by becoming maroons themselves—the quintessential

3.5 Ken-Gar community leader Leonard Jackson shaking
the hand of Montgomery County police officer Melissa Parlon
after his graduation from the Montgomery County Police
Citizen Academy in 1995 (Montgomery County, Maryland,
Department of Police 1995, 6).

example being Queen Nanny of the Windward Maroons of Jamaica—their
reproductive labor responsibilities posed additional challenges to escaping from slavery (Diouf 2014, 90). By contrast, enslaved men often had
more knowledge of the outside world and invited fewer suspicions compared to women, children, and other groups because they were afforded
some limited mobility to travel outside the plantation for errands and other
tasks (Diouf 2014, 89). Maroon geographies have always echoed structures
of racial, sexual, and gender domination even as maroons escape from the
center of those oppressions. Due to maroons' complicated entanglements
with structures of unfreedom, Yarimar Bonilla (2015, 43) explains that marronage itself "represents a form of strategic entanglement: a way of crafting

and enacting autonomy within a system from which one is unable to fully disentangle."

The strategic entanglements of maroon geographies provide lessons for how to adapt to systemic constraints like policing and simultaneously maintain spaces of freedom in contexts of seeming impossibility. In Montgomery County, for example, maroon geographies are characterized by negotiations with state actors that, while replicating existing power relations in some ways, still support residents' resistance to racial violence enacted and supported by the state. Maroon justice does not exist entirely outside the parameters of the state; rather, it models how to achieve justice within the limitations of state sovereignty. Simply put, while maroon geographies extend beyond state and state-sanctioned systems of racial, sexual, gender, and class oppression, they remain in conflict and relation with dominant actors and structures.

The contradictions laden in local adherence to the principles of maroon justice are a reminder that abolition is a process of transformation, not something to be attained at once. Acknowledging how maroon geographies articulate with modes of state governance "in dialectical, or contradictory, and transformational ways" (Sayers 2014, 8) creates space for interrogating and addressing the limitations of present negotiations with power while still centering radical imaginations. The compromises that have made maroon geographies possible are also a warning to consider who is left behind in particular struggles for criminal justice reform and transformation. Struggles for abolition must center everyone as part of a radically expansive conceptualization of community and humanity.

The Transformative Possibilities of Maroon Justice

Overall, an abundance of archival materials and my interviews with community members show strong evidence of alternative community safety and security measures that have helped supplant the need for police intervention in Montgomery County's Black communities. The principles of maroon justice—community-based accountability, the rejection of value systems that hierarchically categorize people when harms occur, and structural solutions to conflict and violence—have long permeated local Black residents' interactions with one another as well as the philosophies of their community institutions. Moreover, despite local Black communities largely embracing increased police involvement during the last quarter of the twentieth century, residents have been able to return to a general environment of autonomy from policing since then. In Lincoln Park, for example, a resident explained that in recent years, she hardly ever sees a police patrol in the neighborhood. The provisional compromises characterizing maroon geographies portend a viable route toward freedom from policing.

In Montgomery County, Maryland, and beyond, maroon justice signals a bold possibility for transforming larger social structures in which harm and violence develop and are reproduced. Beginning with restoring interpersonal relationships and developing community-based structural solutions to prevent harm, maroon justice offers a pathway toward a large-scale project of police abolition. In the following chapter, I explore ways that local Black neighborhoods evidence a possible future world in which policing has been supplanted by alternative definitions and practices of safety and security.

[Marginality is] much more than a site of deprivation. . . . It is also the site of radical possibility, a space of resistance . . . a central location for the production of a counter-hegemonic discourse that is not just found in words but in habits of being and the way one lives. As such, I was not speaking of a marginality one wishes to lose—to give up or surrender as part of moving into the centre—but rather as a site one stays in, clings to even, because it nourishes one's capacity to resist. It offers to one the possibility of radical perspective from which to see and create, to imagine alternatives, new worlds.

bell hooks, "Choosing the Margin as a Space of Radical Openness" (1989)

Maroon geographies signal from the social, political, and physical margins of dominant society a radical praxis of community. In Montgomery County, the Black communities of Haiti, Ken-Gar, Lincoln Park, Sandy Spring, Scotland, Sugarland, and Tobytown are spaces of multigenerational cooperation and interdependence. Since their establishment, they have offered sites of refuge for Black people in a world of racial violence. As previous chapters showed, the history of marronage and later practices of state evasion and maroon justice have been central to the maintenance of safety and security in local Black communities. In this chapter, I explore how safety and security have developed among Black residents through radical practices of community.

Here, the term *community* requires explicit definition. Communities are habitually romanticized—cherished as bastions of "cooperation, equality, and communion" (Joseph 2002, vii)—and fetishized, or treated as "independent, organic entities" without regard for the people and labor that produce them (Joseph 2002, 57). While I use the term throughout this book as a shorthand to name the spatial and social structure of modern-day maroon geographies in my study site, I pause here to delineate a specific definition of community that describes these places. More than a simple designation for a seemingly inevitable grouping of people within a place, community is "a never-ending process of being together, of struggling over the boundaries and substance of togetherness, and of coproducing this togetherness in complex relations of power" (Gibson-Graham et al. 2017, 5). Montgomery County's maroon geographies are sites of community intentionally crafted by Black residents to resist domination and exploitation by the white society surrounding them.

Many community formations—like Montgomery County at large—serve to reinforce the social hierarchies and boundaries central to racial capitalism. The universalizing power of community helps conceal and legitimize the operations of racism, heterosexism, and other oppressions required for capitalist exploitation. The unequal rights of access and privilege associated with belonging to a particular community are solidified in practices of enclosure and border making. In this way, community building often reinscribes capitalist property relations and the policing of who belongs or does not belong within a community's collective subjecthood. Without attention to the social relations and labor undergirding a community's creation and reproduction, the language of "community" obscures the "exclusionary and disciplining characteristics" that often undergird it (Joseph 2002, xxi).

The open-ended and complex nature of community, along with its romanticization as a social and spatial locus of belonging and protection, also inspires its appropriation. As Neil Smith (1992, 70) elucidates, "Community is . . . the least specifically defined of spatial scales, and the consequent vagueness yet generally affirmative, nurturing meaning attached to 'community' makes it one of the most ideologically appropriated metaphors in contemporary public discourse. From 'the community of nations' fighting a murderous war against Iraq, to 'the business community' attempting to justify class-based exploitation, the idea of community is appropriated to rescript less salubrious realities." "Community" policing is one of the latest and most highly celebrated appropriations of the idea—with a variety of actors, including police officers, government officials, scholars, and church leaders supporting the rescripting of community as a police-made panacea to crime, racial police violence, and resistance to policing (Hansford 2016,

215). Given the ostensible location of "community" outside of the state, community policing works to simultaneously enable and conceal state control at the local scale (Story 2019, 139).

Community policing, which originated in the 1960s, comprises a set of practices whereby police attempt to gain trust and encourage cooperation from the policed through tacking onto their roles what are thought of as benign ways to build relationships with residents. Community policing is also touted as a way to reduce police violence by helping police officers shake their fear of working-class Black neighborhoods and other hyper-criminalized places. From cops hosting "Sweet Tea Days" in Black neighborhoods (Hansford 2016, 216) to delivering bifocals to elderly residents of housing projects (Gilmore and Gilmore 2016, 181), however, community policing initiatives negatively impact residents by further entrenching police presence in their everyday lives. Moreover, in working to bolster relationships between residents and police and encouraging more residents to rely on police, community policing initiatives are designed to fragment the forms of community that keep people from calling the police in the first place. A case in point are programs that invite residents to allow police officers to conduct surveillance of their fellow neighbors from inside their homes (Montgomery County, Maryland, Department of Police 1993). Community policing is thus a tool to preserve the institutional dominance of policing through an appropriation and rupture—rather than an actual embodiment—of community.

In a long era shaped by violent appropriations of the notion of community, the term still points to spaces of radical potential. Under the banner of community, for example, organizers in Baltimore established the Community Conferencing Center in 2000 to provide city residents with alternatives to police, including conflict intervention and educational and counseling programs (Maher 2021). While the organization now goes by Restorative Response Baltimore, it continues to use the term *community conferencing* to describe its restorative justice space and to structure dialogue facilitation for people involved in and impacted by conflict or harm (Restorative Response Baltimore, n.d.). More broadly, the scale of community encompassing people living and working in close proximity to each other can engender local organizing efforts that displace police. One illustration of this is the establishment of temporary "No Cop Zones" in West Philadelphia where people came together to communicate their experiences with police, discuss alternatives to police, and imagine a world without them

(Maher 2021). Hence, as much as the carceral state employs community as "an ideological strategy of legitimation," community remains an important "geographic site for action" to transform carceral power (Story 2019, 140).

In Montgomery County's maroon geographies, community takes place through daily, grounded practices of care and cooperation beyond policing. Instead of relying on agents of the state to ensure their safety and sense of security, community members engage with one another to shape their built and social environments in ways that preclude the need for routine police intervention in their neighborhoods. They look out for their neighbors, practice cooperative living strategies, and work together to delineate how state resources come to shape their neighborhoods. Local Black communities demonstrate how community can take place beyond policing and illuminate the kind of biological, productive, and reproductive possibilities afforded by not calling the police.

The radical Black praxis of community in Montgomery County is rooted in the history of slavery and racial segregation as well as an oppositional politics of marronage. Spatial segregation and flight from slavery gave rise to these Black autonomous spaces, and the continuously isolated environments and strong social ties between residents serve as mediums through which residents have expressed and enacted their visions of community. For early residents, these communities began as places where life could be defined beyond the confines of dominant society—they were places where their children were born as humans rather than chattel, places where their lives held value outside the order of racial capitalism. Later residents maintained a level of self-determinacy built upon conditions reproduced for their own negation. Their ongoing abandonment by the state required Black residents to develop livelihoods and epistemologies of care outside the register of state violence. Referencing the local Black community of Scotland, for example, a 1975 Montgomery County Human Relations Commission memorandum concluded with the following observation: "That community is more determined to do for itself than any community I know of. All the county could and should do is stand by and be available" ("Memorandum" 1975). Scotland and the wider constellation of maroon geographies in Montgomery County demonstrate how enclosure and isolation might operate as conditions for freedom instead of discipline and exclusion.

In this chapter, I explore the social production of the radical Black praxis of community shaping maroon geographies in Montgomery County. I argue that this praxis is a model for a world liberated from policing. In place of reforms like community policing, radical Black epistemologies and practices of community sustain rather than disrupt relationships of care undergirding safety and security. This radical praxis of community helps dismantle the notion that police are necessary, or even useful, for the maintenance of safe, healthy communities.

Fostering Environments of Care

Care is central to the praxis of community in Montgomery County's historically Black neighborhoods. Care is an ethical practice, politics, and attitude that encompasses regard for one's own and others' well-being and protection (Tronto 1993; Till 2012). In previous chapters, I touched upon the idea that care is essential to ending policing. From the witnesses who mobilized their bodies (and shoes) in attempts to save Thomas Broadus and Carolyn Twyman from death by police to the community-based accountability systems practiced in Montgomery County's historically Black communities, acts of care create openings for imagining alternatives to police. Everyday acts of care demonstrate not only how to respond to and challenge policing but also how to construct "new forms of relationships, institutions, and action that enhance mutuality and well-being" (Lawson 2007, 8).

Geographers drawing on feminist understandings of the interrelated processes of social reproduction and the production of space have theorized care as a critical part of transforming spaces to create a more just world (e.g., Gibson-Graham 2006; Lawson 2007; Till 2012; M. Williams 2017). For example, J. K. Gibson-Graham (2006, 33) argues that when routine acts of care—in which people share their time, money, material resources, and affection—are centered and acknowledged, the "apparent rationality" of capitalism seems "less legitimate, less 'natural,' and less able to dominate." In other words, a consideration of everyday practices of care can help people envision themselves as already in the process of becoming postcapitalist subjects. Likewise, an attentiveness to the routine practice and politics of care in Black communities in Montgomery County highlights the existence of nonpolice forms of safety and security that can inform abolitionist organizing. A focus on care also requires a recognition of the labor of people of color, women, working-class people, and immigrants, who bear a disproportionate amount of the care work that sustains the world. Places shaped by these marginal groups are animated by radical care practices that portend police-free futures.

The "place-based ethics of care" (Till 2012, 8) shaping local maroon geographies is founded in practices of attending to and caring for the Earth as the basis of community. In escaping and creating life beyond slavery, early residents of Black communities in Montgomery County developed relationships with the Earth beyond conquest and continuous extraction. Earth, for them, was not merely a means for property ownership and profit; rather, they cared for the Earth so that it could provide sustenance to them and serve as a haven for themselves and their families. Their place-based care ethic was similar to that of Jamaican maroons, who organized their communities around what Sylvia Wynter (1970, 37) termed a "provision ground ideology," which centers the Earth as "the base of the community, and . . . the common good." It also embodies more widespread "abolition ecologies" (Heynen and Ybarra 2021) created through everyday efforts by oppressed people to push up against the human and environmental exploitations of colonialism, slavery, racial capitalism, and carcerality by building land-based, life-affirming practices and institutions. By caring for the Earth, residents of Montgomery County's maroon geographies were able to produce and maintain a grounded practice of community that included direct alternatives to policing as well as broad practices of collectivity such as communal landownership and subsistence gardening. While the connection between police abolition and these latter examples of care may not be immediately apparent, I argue that they enable residents to counteract the violence of policing in their communities by reconfiguring dominant arrangements of state governance and racial capitalism.

Across local Black communities, residents shared with me examples of cooperative living strategies that undergirded relationships of care and that allowed residents to maintain safety and security beyond policing. For example, the eschewing of private, individual land ownership in favor of collective, community-defined land tenure enabled Black community members to use land not as a means for financial gain but as a material and fugitive infrastructure for care. Residents often shared parcels of land, subdividing their properties between family members and neighbors (Porter 1988). In addition, because many Black residents were skeptical of government involvement in their home lives, they did not always follow official procedures for recording and transferring property ownership. For example, Black residents living in Sandy Spring systematically refused to file deeds to their properties because they were afraid to attract the attention of the local government (Porter 1988). Likewise, Scotland residents did not often designate land to particular descendants in their wills, and consequently the community did not have clear land titles (Siegel 1973). Practices such as this reflected residents' dismissal of capitalist principles of land ownership such as the protection of private property—a key function of modern police in the United States. Without clearly defined private property, residents neither needed nor invited its protection by the state.

The physical environments that residents built reinforced their shared, community-based understandings of land. In Haiti, for example, "fences, alleys, and other natural boundaries did not defensively proclaim individual ownership"; instead, property lines were unclear and land appeared as "community property" (Maryland Historical Trust, n.d., section 7, p. 4). Moreover, the open, communal landscapes in local Black communities served as a material negation of carceral geographies: "fences, walls, hedgerows, and other boundary structures were generally used to contain and control livestock rather than people" (Maryland Historical Trust, n.d., section 7, p. 4). This collective approach to land ownership contributed to close relationships between neighbors. For example, a Haiti resident born in the 1930s recalled that as a child, "everyone was 'family,' directly related or not, and every door was literally open. . . . In his youth he never knocked on the door of any house in the community but opened it and entered as if it were his own" (Maryland Historical Trust, n.d., section 7, p. 4). Likewise, a Lincoln Park resident, Sharyn Duffin, explained to me that in her youth, "everybody knew who lived here, and you could sleep with your doors open, I mean literally open not just unlocked." Residents of Sandy Spring and Tobytown also characterize their youth as an age of unlocked and open doors.

Other noncapitalist practices that fostered safe, healthy Black communities in Montgomery County included subsistence strategies. From the founding of local Black communities, residents cultivated gardens and raised livestock: "By working their land, they provided the basic foodstuffs from garden produce, orchards, and animals so that their families could survive and perhaps come out a little ahead by bartering their surplus. As they had during slavery, the founders depended upon one another and upon themselves. They helped neighbors to build their own houses, clear their land, butcher animals, and preserve the meat" (McDaniel 1979c, 155). Such modes of subsistence made local Black communities "fundamentally intractable to state appropriation" (J. C. Scott 2009, 6). While the United States developed an economy that profited from the labor, servitude, and consumption needs of workers ranging from enslaved people on plantations to postslavery wage laborers, Black community members in Montgomery County established relative autonomy from these exploitations.

In Sandy Spring, a resident explained to me that everyone took on a specific role for the community so that all needs were met:

> My grandfather used to have a huge garden. He would share what he grew. . . . Granddaddy always . . . planted enough stuff to feed Sandy Spring. . . . But the people in this community, everybody did something different as far as their job was concerned. But they were willing to share with each other if they had an excess of something. They would share. "Take this down to Miss Lena. She may need this," for example. My grandmother was a seamstress, so if anybody got lots of fabric or got something, they would give it to Mama Lena because she was the one that did all the sewing in the community. That kind of thing. My aunt who lived in one of the other houses, for example, made cookies. So she'd make cookies for the community. Everybody knew that Aunt Louise was going to make cookies for Christmas. This little area here was sort of close knit. So everybody knew that that's what she did for Christmas. It was like we were in our own little kingdom kind of thing.

In Lincoln Park, a group of men even worked together to move a house to a vacant lot in the neighborhood when a woman and her children wanted to move to Lincoln Park after purchasing a home. Reflecting on this community moment, a resident said to me: "I don't know what they used or how they did it, but they moved that house for her. It's just a matter of everybody just helped each other. It was a struggle, and there was a feeling that you had to stick together, for all of us to get something done."

One subsistence strategy that residents repeatedly told me was a key expression of the collectivity underscoring community safety and security was communal pig butchering. While not still done today, communal pig butchering was practiced as recently as the mid-twentieth century in local Black communities. In an interview with me, Eddie Dove explained how it worked in Scotland:

> Everybody helped each other. . . . And back in the wintertime, the people that raised hogs, they butchered in November. And the men would go around and help each other. And if I butchered my hog today, anybody lived down the road, up the road, somewhere in the fork of the road somewhere, if you had any hogs, you would butcher yours too. And we would help each other. I would go to your house and help you butcher your hog, put 'em on

a pole and skin it and all whatnot. And the next day, you would come to my house and have meat.

Likewise, in Lincoln Park, pig butchering was an all-day affair during which neighbors came and helped the person doing the butchering. "Everybody would just chip in and help," explained a Lincoln Park resident. Residents in Sugarland, Sandy Spring, and Haiti also butchered pigs and shared the meat with neighbors. Communal pig butchering and other subsistence strategies allowed members of Black communities to maintain networks of support and to quite literally secure the survival of their communities.

On an institutional level, churches and community organizations played a key role in fostering a strong sense of community and supporting social reproduction. In Scotland, the African Methodist Episcopal (AME) Zion Church's Ministry of Kindness, for example, helped residents in need by doing such things as paying their rent when they lacked funds, giving them money to pay for food, and helping take care of sick people. Scotland residents also developed a service called HELP that aided people in the case of emergencies (Curtis 1972). In addition, residents across Black communities were members of Black benevolent societies such as the Order of the Galilean Fishermen, an organization first created in Baltimore in 1856 that covered expenses for the ill, widows, and funerals prior to insurance being made commercially available to Black people. A local chapter was established in 1912. Mutual aid societies and churches have been cornerstones of Black community life across the United States since the late eighteenth century.

The sense of collectivity and the relationships of care and support between members of Black communities in Montgomery County have enabled residents to maintain their safety and security beyond policing. Current and former residents explained that the maintenance of safety and security in their communities was a task for themselves and their neighbors, not law enforcement. Lincoln Park resident Anita Summerour told me that she has always felt "very safe" in her neighborhood because neighbors watch out for one another. She explained: "You came to know your neighbor's habit, whether they went out to work, whether they were home all day. And sometimes people would say, 'I'm going out. Would you watch my house?' So it was just all of us helping each other. . . . A lot of the people in the community were related to each other, and even if we weren't, you watched out for your neighbor's house." Similarly, June Johnson, who grew up in Sandy Spring and has spent her entire life there, explained that "everybody looked out for everybody else and . . . everybody knew everybody in the community." She further described how her late father, Thomas Eugene "Babe" Snowden Jr., served as a security monitor for everyone in the neighborhood until he passed away in 2018. He dedicated his time to observing activities in the neighborhood and would call to alert neighbors if unknown visitors were approaching their homes or if he witnessed anything out of the ordinary. June and her family members used to jokingly tell people that they don't have ADT (an electronic security monitoring and alarm system) but that they had B.A.B.E.—the letters of her father's nickname. The embedded role of these everyday safety and security practices in the traditions of socioeconomic cooperation demonstrates the interdependent relationship between alternatives to capitalism and alternatives to police.

Because their communities offered almost everything that they needed to sustain and reproduce life, residents were able to partly insulate themselves from routine violence on the part of the racial capitalist state. Across generations, residents passed down collective practices and arrangements of community that encouraged radical care, cooperation, and trust in each other rather than reliance on police. This collectivity characterizes maroon geographies in general. Like Black community members across Montgomery County, maroons throughout the western hemisphere and communities that supported slavery's fugitives developed thriving subsistence livelihoods; they hunted, raised hogs and fowl, foraged for fruits and herbs, grew produce, and built shelter and transport means (Price 1996; Diouf 2014). They also established their own safety and security measures in order to isolate themselves from the slave economy and prevent crossing paths with slave patrollers (Diouf 2014).

The collectivity of maroon geographies exemplifies how community safety and security can be secured outside of policing. Even during periods of heightened policing and issues in their neighborhoods, many residents sustained their community-based approach to safety and security. In the midst of the drug crisis in Lincoln Park in the 1980s and 1990s when the East Rockville Community Action Team was active, for example, community members often turned to one another rather than the police to express frustration with and learn about what was going on. A Lincoln Park resident told me that residents would sit on each other's front porches to have conversations about the drug problem and observe activities in the neighborhood. She believed that these "nosy" neighbor porch sessions helped deter people involved in using and selling drugs because "they knew we were watching." Moreover, many residents did not allow criminalizing stigmas to diminish their trust in their neighbors. Joe Davis, a longtime resident of Lincoln Park, told the *Rockville Express* newspaper in 1991 (during the height of Lincoln Park's drug-related police initiatives): "I love Lincoln Park, that's all. . . . It's a wonderful community where you can walk out of your house, not lock your door and no one will bother you" (Stieff 1991). Similarly, when interviewed by a *Washington Post* reporter in 1999, Ken-Gar resident Joseph Woods explained, "Even in Ken-Gar's worst years . . . 'We were never burglarized. I've always felt safe enough to leave my door un-latched'" (Mitric 1999).

Importantly, Montgomery County's Black communities are not spaces of vigilantism or self-policing but refuges from the logics of policing. Residents have developed and maintained strong relationships with one another centered on trust, care, and support—not surveillance and crime prevention. As a resident of one Black community in Montgomery County stated: "It was a togetherness project" (McDaniel 1979b). June Johnson, of Sandy Spring, summarized the general sense of safety and security derived from her close-knit community: "I've never felt unsafe here. I've never felt unsafe all my life here. The idea of taking extra precautions for safety, has never, ever been something that I've ever dwelled on."

Divesting from Police and Investing in Community Needs

A significant, contemporary example of the local Black praxis of community in Montgomery County is the conversion of former police infrastructure into community-run space in Lincoln Park. Nestled just on the other side of the Washington Metrorail tracks from the Montgomery County seat in downtown Rockville, Lincoln Park was ground zero for the local government's first community policing initiative. The "Lincoln Park/First Street Neighborhood Empowerment Initiative"—which later was bluntly termed the "Lincoln Park Drug Initiative"—was jointly initiated in 1988 by the Montgomery County and Rockville City police departments, along-side the county and city governments, to combat drug-related activity in the neighborhood (Montgomery County, Maryland, Department of Police 1989). The switch in terminology from the neighborhood empowerment-focused original name to the Lincoln Park Drug Initiative exemplifies the program's prioritization of law and order over community. Lincoln Park had developed a reputation as an "open-air" drug market due to an increase in the usage and sale of crack cocaine during the late 1980s (Montgomery

County, Maryland, Department of Police 1993). Community policing was put forth as a tool to reduce drug-related crime, improve "quality of life," and promote a "positive climate of trust and cooperation" between police and residents in Lincoln Park (Montgomery County, Maryland, Department of Police 1993).

As part of the community policing initiative in Lincoln Park, a police substation was installed in a converted public housing apartment owned by the City of Rockville Housing Authority. Like the change in the initiative's name, the elimination of public housing to make room for police infrastructure in Lincoln Park exposes how the priority of community policing is not to build and maintain community but to enable closer, more intimate surveillance and policing of residents. In 1990, the substation was moved to a house purchased by the City of Rockville so that it could be closer to the Lincoln Park Community Center, the hub of the neighborhood's activities (Nurmi 1991). The substation eventually became an attachment to the community center, which is governed and funded by the City of Rockville.

In 2012, Lincoln Park residents successfully converted the police substation into a community-operated tutoring and mentoring space. The conversion was led by the Lincoln Park Community Center director, who asked the Rockville Police Department to turn over the substation for use as a community space because she saw no need for physical police infrastructure in the community. In fact, the police substation had been slowly transforming into a community space over the years since its use by police had significantly declined by the early 2000s. Residents very rarely called the police, and the neighborhood was generally quiet (Lincoln Park Civic Association, n.d.). Given the lack of a need for dedicated police space, the community center staff had installed a refrigerator in the substation and were using some of the space for storage. The community center director even had a key to the substation while it was still in use by police. Wanting to fully take advantage of the opportunity to have more space of their own, the Lincoln Park Community Center director had the usage officially changed and the police removed to their headquarters in downtown Rockville.

In its new role as a tutoring and mentoring space, the former police substation was filled with educational materials for neighborhood children and desk space for volunteer tutors and mentors (figure 4.1). There are books donated from the Montgomery County Public School system, and the space has been used for Lincoln Park youth programs as well as a summer mentorship program run by the City of Rockville's Community Services

4.1 Inside the Lincoln Park Community Center, a former police substation, 2018. Photograph by author.

Department. This transformation of space in the Lincoln Park Community Center offers an example for how to divest from police forces and invest in human needs like education and mentorship.

Crucially, the tutoring and mentoring efforts that replaced police presence did not reify the logics of community policing by inviting police further into residents' lives simply in new roles as tutors and mentors. Such an approach to community policing, in fact, was used in Tobytown in 2001 through a program funded by a Montgomery County Housing Opportunities Commission drug elimination grant in which the community's children were tutored twice a week by police officers stationed in the community (Wraga 2001b).[1] Instead, the conversion of the police substation in Lincoln Park was a truly nonpolice, community-based effort that demonstrates that safety and security mean something much more complex and far-reaching than reforms of policing. Safety and security require turning away from police and turning toward community institutions of support and care.

In their flight from policing to education, Lincoln Park residents echo a common call in abolitionist movements to divest from policing and invest in public services like education (Center for Popular Democracy, Law for

Black Lives, and Black Youth Project 100 2017; Movement for Black Lives [M4BL] 2020c). In order for such investments to support Black liberation, it is critical to extend abolition to schooling in order to dismantle the policies and practices that position spaces of education within carceral racial regimes (Sojoyner 2016; Stovall 2018; Movement for Black Lives [M4BL] 2020c). The Lincoln Park police substation conversion models a transformative approach to education by creating a public, nonpolice, community-based site of education in a historically forgotten Black community.

The conversion of the police substation at the Lincoln Park Community Center illustrates how state resources can be shifted from governance as criminalization to the funding of social programs that benefit a community. The community center is still funded by the City of Rockville. In addition, a 2021 Maryland Legislative Bond Initiative sponsored by Maryland state senator Cheryl C. Kagan requested $250,000 in state funding for further reconfiguring the former substation space to make it better suited for community programming and gatherings (Maryland General Assembly 2021). This example of divestment from police infrastructure demonstrates how the state might be used as a tool for police abolition. A program of police abolition could systematize the type of state resource transformation that brought an end to the police substation in Lincoln Park. In this way, state power can be used to secure human needs.

Of course, mobilizing state agents and resources to help end policing mandates "a radical reimagination of the state and the law that serves it" (Akbar 2018, 479). It requires shrinking the state's law enforcement apparatus and investing in state infrastructure and resources that support employment, affordable and safe housing, education, health care, and other basic needs. My call for such a redistribution of resources echoes the demands of activists over centuries. Just as enslaved and free Black people in the nineteenth century demanded freedom, equal citizenship rights, and mass land redistribution—what W. E. B. Du Bois ([1935] 1998) termed "abolition-democracy"—organizers today demand divestments from police and prisons and public investments instead in Black communities (see Movement for Black Lives [M4BL] 2020a). What will make this equitable redistribution of resources possible is a radical reconstruction of governance.

Divestments from policing require an upheaval of the imperatives that first produced the nation-state as a scale of social and political organization for capitalism. Prior to the emergence of capitalism, state power was conferred at the urban or regional scales; the scale of the modern nation-state was subsequently created to fulfill the need for an expansive range of governance that could support an emergent capitalism's extensive economic activity and accumulation beginning in the sixteenth century (Smith 1992, 75). With the further development of capitalism, the state has remained integral to the functions and dominance of the capitalist market economy. Micol Seigel (2018, 19) uses the term *state-market* to name "the structuring matrix capitalism provides for the state, and vice-versa." In its supporting role for capitalism, the state institutionalizes "exploitation and oppression on the basis of class, race, gender, and other social differences" to secure the interests of the ruling class, and it polices those who threaten the state-market's legitimacy (Smith 1992, 75). Police abolition therefore requires upending the state-market formation. Despite the capitalist state being the only nation-state ever known, Seigel posits, it may not be the only one that can be imagined (2018, 20).[2] Understanding the state as a set of social relations and capacities—as opposed to a singular body with transcendent imperatives—helps illuminate how state power can assist in remaking the state itself.

The state apparatus provides openings, due to its contradictions, to challenge prevailing state logics and violence. The "diffuse and ambiguously defined" substance of the state, which manifests in the "incoherence of state practice" (Mitchell 1999, 76), offers an opportunity to deconstruct existing state formations. Indeed, by making public resources work for them rather than in the service of violent governance, Lincoln Park residents took advantage of the incoherence of the state. They successfully conscripted the state in reducing its own power, thereby loosening the grip of social control in their community. The Lincoln Park substation conversion, however, is also a cautionary example of how police power can be strengthened at the same time that state transformations curtail one form of policing.

The transformation of the police substation in Lincoln Park in 2012 was paradoxically made possible in part by the expansion of local police capacities and the consequent contradictions of local police infrastructure development. The same year that Lincoln Park residents were able to take over the police substation for themselves, a new police headquarters (figure 4.2) opened in downtown Rockville as the culmination of a $6.4 million project designed to accommodate the current police force and allow for 10 percent growth (City of Rockville Planning Commission 2013). Formerly a US Postal Service office, the space for the new police headquarters was deeded at no cost to the City of Rockville by the federal government "with the stipulation that the building would be permanently used for a Homeland Security-related purpose" (City of Rockville Planning Commission 2013).

4.2 Site of Rockville Police Department headquarters, opened in a former US Postal Service office in 2012. Photograph by Evan Kalish.

This cutback from federal resources in the form of postal service, along with a simultaneous devolution of state responsibilities—in the form of "homeland security"—to local government epitomizes what Ruth Wilson Gilmore and Craig Gilmore (2007, 152) call the neoliberal, "anti-state state." This neoliberal state configuration sustains its power by denouncing "big" government—cutting taxes for the wealthy, reducing government oversight of industry, and shrinking social safety nets and services—while expanding the carceral and military operations of the state. In efforts to manage the growing dearth of public safety nets like welfare and health care, the anti-state state mobilizes police as first responders—and substitutes for real solutions—to housing insecurity, school safety needs, and mental health and substance use crises.

But while "community" policing is the name given to legitimize the increased role of police in people's everyday lives, community forms a site of radical potential as a space "where people encounter the political and economic structures that produce and uphold the social order" (Story 2019, 140). In fact, the anti-state state has an ongoing need to innovate: "New, community-based instruments of social and geographic control signal a crisis of legitimacy for the carceral state. . . . This suggests that, in the spaces of transference between one mode of carceral control and another, there is also organizing potential. The community, after all, is also where everyday life is reproduced, and thus also where people will fight to survive and work to be free" (Story 2019, 165–66). In the context of Rockville in 2012, the anti-state state produced a contradiction ripe with the radical possibility for rethinking and organizing community beyond policing. With the opening of the new police headquarters, Lincoln Park residents were able to convince the police department that it no longer needed the space in their community. This development in police infrastructure allowed local residents to combat the intimate policing of their neighborhood and to reinforce an idea that has been held for generations across local Black communities: that police are more harmful than helpful in ensuring community safety and security.

The coincidence of the Lincoln Park police substation conversion and the expansion of local police infrastructure demonstrates how a project of police abolition might appropriate state resources without replicating the structural violence of the state and its linkages with racial capitalism. While policing operates as an ever-morphing "fix" to resolve crises of state legitimacy in the midst of neoliberal political-economic restructuring, maroon geographies are a different type of "spatial fix" (Harvey 2001). Instead of attending to and thereby prolonging the catastrophes innate to racial capitalism by expanding and reorganizing the structure itself, maroon geographies mark a rupture in this process of producing space. In Lincoln Park, the work of residents to convert their neighborhood's police substation into an education space—predicated on the absence of police—reverses the trend by which police increasingly absorb public funds from and substitute for real public services. This radically opposes the anti-state's efforts to resolve the crisis of shrinking public safety nets by investing in expanded roles for police.

Members of historically Black communities throughout Montgomery County have long taken advantage of contradictions inherent in the development and expansion of the racial capitalist state to create environments of collectivity, care, and trust. Neglect by the state and industries of their home communities dating from slavery until the present day has been a major factor requiring local Black residents to organize communities that, while nested within the US nation-state, are still relatively free from policing. The marginality resulting from this neglect has made the "institutional rationalities" (Simone 2004, 410) of the capitalist mode of production—one of which is the necessity of police—untenable in Montgomery County's historically Black communities, and it has inspired and incubated radically capacious definitions and practices of community safety and security beyond policing. This praxis of community lays the groundwork for organizing police abolition in the context of a radically transformed state formation.

The Enduring Radical Black Praxis of Community

The value of care that local Black residents have fostered among each other and shaped into the built environments of their communities has endured. Even with demographic shifts—including Black families emigrating from the South and internationally, and settling in the communities over time, as well as growing Latine, Asian, and white presence (Magruder 1976; Hill 1991; Burns 1992)—many new residents have taken on prevailing epistemologies and practices of community. As older residents have passed away, as the descendants of multigenerational families have moved away, and as newcomers have moved in, local Black neighborhoods remain places where community is defined and lived beyond policing. Such endurance of the local praxis of community has been made possible, in part, through the ways that "identities established at other scales are . . . rolled into struggles over community" (Smith 1992, 70). In other words, different racial and ethnic groups have converged through shared political struggles for community well-being.

Remaining long-term residents and later arrivals work together to keep alive radical Black definitions and practices of safety and security. In Lincoln Park, for example, the community center director who led the conversion of the police substation to a tutoring and mentoring space is the daughter of a Ghanaian immigrant. After moving to Lincoln Park, she would sit with community elders to listen to their stories of the "good old days" beginning from the histories of resistance to and flight from slavery. She also absorbed the trust and sense of safety and security that residents had in Lincoln Park. For example, she learned from former Lincoln Park resident Bobby Israel, who used to work with her at the community center, that he always kept the doors to his home and car unlocked. In an interview with me, the community center director recounted:

> Mr. Israel, he, up until the day he passed, he never locked his doors. Never. Even in the '80s and '90s, 2000s. He just never . . . His thing was, "If you're

going to break into my car, just open the door and get what you need and go." You know, "I don't want to pay for a new window." So, and then he just had that trust in his community and didn't want to feel the need that he had to change that. And I thought that was pretty cool, to still have that sense of security and trust in your community. And he still talked about the times people went in his car and got stuff. But it didn't make him change his ways. He still . . . didn't lock his door. . . . Regardless of what was going on, he never felt the need to change his safety. He didn't want to feel that he couldn't be safe in his community. So he didn't change that.

The Lincoln Park Civic Association (LPCA) president and vice president in 2018 were also immigrants—the former is from Nigeria and the latter from Réunion. These Lincoln Park leaders have helped maintain the robust sense of community that they inherited as newcomers to the neighborhood. The mission of the LPCA is precisely "to foster a strong sense of community; to promote shared interests in preserving and maintaining Lincoln Park's historical character; and to encourage neighborhood involvement in efforts to enhance the well being of its residents" (Lincoln Park Civic Association 2016, 1).

Likewise, other historically Black communities in Montgomery County have shared with newcomers multigenerational practices of community beyond policing. A Sandy Spring resident who moved to the community when he was twenty-five years old, for example, explained to me that residents initially "were private, but they were also very eager to help you or support you if you need something. That kind of thing . . . it's just a strong sense of community." After settling in Sandy Spring, he developed close relationships with his neighbors that have allowed him to feel a sense of safety and security without police. He has never had to call the police during the forty-seven years he has lived in Sandy Spring, and he once intervened in a dispute between two neighbors so that the police did not have to get involved. He explained that he tried to resolve things because he "just didn't think it was that worthy of that level" of calling the police.

Lifelong residents also continue to trust their neighbors. Fran Hawkins, for example, assured me that protections like iron bars are still unnecessary in Lincoln Park. Likewise, a Scotland resident told me: "I bet I can go twenty-four hours a day, year-round without locking my door. Not worry about anything. . . . I've seen people leave lawnmowers and tools and whatnot, left right on their pickup truck. Nobody bothered it. We don't have break-ins over there. Nope." This Scotlander's faith in his neighbors echoes Lincoln Park resident Joe Davis's trust in his fellow neighbors when he went out of town in 1950 and left his house unlocked for two weeks with a brand new television sitting inside. When he returned, nothing had been touched (Stieff 1991).

Of course, there are challenges to maintaining the sense of community undergirding residents' trust in each other and their rejection of policing. In fact, as early as the 1990s, some residents began locking their doors in reaction to changes such as the drug crisis surrounding Black communities and the disruptions of urban renewal. For example, Clarice Williams, who had spent her whole life in Tobytown when she was interviewed at sixty-eight years old about the outcome of the neighborhood's urban renewal project in 1991, said that she was beginning to lock her doors "sometimes" after a lifetime of keeping her doors unlocked (Wagner 1991). Likewise, in Lincoln Park, Gladys Hubbard said that things changed in the 1990s during the neighborhood's drug crisis: "Everybody's got all kinds of locks on their doors now" (Phelps 1991).

Moreover, as ties between neighbors have weakened over time and as older residents have passed away or moved on, some residents have increased their reliance on police. One Lincoln Park resident, for example, sends an email with emergency contact information to the police chief when she goes on trips. In the past, however, she did not rely on police because she had a neighbor who watched over her property even when she was in town: "I had a neighbor who knew everything . . . more of what was going on at my house than I did. I knew if we went away, he would take a daily walk around my house. . . . He did it for my household because I've known him since I was a child. He and my father were best friends." With the departure of former residents, it has become increasingly difficult to maintain informal systems of safety and security that were once in place, and there is consequently more reliance on formal policing.

Overall, however, a radically collective praxis of community remains strong in historically Black communities in Montgomery County. When I asked a Sandy Spring resident what lessons her community offers for safety and security on a larger scale, she directly referred to this sense of collectivity:

> The "communical" kind of attitude that doesn't exist outside of the family kind of community that you have here—outside the Black community. Looking out for one another, being observant of what's going on, communicating with one another, letting people know when you're going out of town, when you're not gonna be in town, you know if there's something going on

in your community that's not right, that's not safe. That's what we would do here. . . . But that's something that's not just prevalent here, I think, it's in all of the Black communities probably throughout the country but especially if you're talking about Montgomery County and this area because I know many of the people in other communities. My husband had an aunt who lived in Lincoln Park. Poolesville, Haiti, Scotland, all of those old small clusters of Black people. That's the kind of thing people did. They looked out for each other; they looked out for each other's property and that kind of thing.

There's No Community in Policing

The radical Black praxis of community emanating from Montgomery County's historically Black communities is a pivotal deviation from the misnomer of "community policing" and other reformist reforms. There is no community in policing, and, as Geo Maher remarks, "there is no abolition without community" (2021, 140). While community policing merely gives lip service to the notion of "community" in order to reify the police state, Black epistemologies and practices of community have allowed residents in Montgomery County to restructure power relations between themselves and the state. Black community members have taken advantage of their marginality and have successfully drawn upon state resources in order to promote an abolitionist vision of community.

Members of Montgomery County's historically Black communities form an infrastructure of safety and security that precludes any consistent need for police intervention. The phrase "people as infrastructure" has been mobilized by AbdouMaliq Simone (2004, 411) as a signifier of the richly heterogeneous spaces of economic and cultural production in Johannesburg, South Africa, where marginalized residents collaborate with one another to "derive maximal outcomes from a minimal set of elements." The concept can also be translated to the context of small, predominately Black communities located on the periphery of the US capital, where residents developed cooperative living strategies in order to survive and reproduce life on their own terms. In these communities, residents continue to embody the radical notion that community safety and security are best ensured through nonpolice mechanisms such as community services, cooperation, and relationship building. What allows residents to live in their neighborhoods without fearing for their safety and what gives them a sense of security is simply each other.

The story of Black community laid out here and in previous chapters illuminates the possibility of a world without police. In the places where marronage and racial autonomy defined the early parameters of Black life and placemaking, the practice of flight from and holding ground outside of racial and economic violence continues to shape abolitionist community building. The radical Black praxis of community in Montgomery County is not limited by tight geographic boundaries or particular subjectivities. Even while isolating themselves from state and state-sanctioned racial violence, Black residents sustain relationships with other local neighborhoods that suggest how the politics of abolition transcend geographically contiguous actors. On a larger scale, the global appropriation of "community" by police shows how particular formations of community can transcend all sorts of borders. If we must take any lesson from community policing, let it be that. In an analogous way, profoundly expansive definitions and practices of community beyond policing can be located and cultivated globally throughout different geographic contexts and among diverse sets of people. The following chapter explores how the commitments and goals of marronage are echoed in Black struggles against police violence in the United States and across the globe. I draw lessons from maroon geographies for policymaking to scale up such examples of community beyond policing.

5   Maroon Geographies and the Paradox of Abolition Policy

In 2020, organizing against police violence grew to a scale never before reached. Millions of people in the United States and worldwide coalesced to protest persistent police brutality amid a different, overlapping pandemic: COVID-19. As the virus causing COVID-19 spread around the globe, it quickly became clear that systemic inequities in areas such as health care, employment, housing, and carceral systems caused Black people and other racial and ethnic minority groups to face heightened vulnerabilities to contracting and dying from the virus (Alexander, Allo, and Klukoff 2020; Rozenfeld et al. 2020; Webb Hooper, Nápoles, and Pérez-Stable 2020). Alongside the COVID-19 threat, police continued to increase the risk of premature death for these groups. In the United States, the police who murdered Breonna Taylor and George Floyd in March and May 2020, respectively, put a spotlight on how policing intersects with other forms of routine racial violence that shorten Black lives. Following Taylor's and Floyd's deaths and the police killings of other Black people globally, organizing for police abolition reverberated throughout the world. Across the United States, organizers' wins in 2020 included an $840 million reduction in police department expenditures, the removal of police officers from schools in more than twenty-five cities, increased transparency and public control over budgets, and $160 million in new community investments (Interrupting Criminalization 2020). These currents of activism carry on the momentum of expansive and long-term abolitionist struggles animating maroon geographies, which have always defied policing, confinement, and other structures of anti-Black violence.

Police abolition comprises a radical vision and praxis of world building. By recognizing the impossibility of police reform to stop police violence, police abolitionists work to end policing through developing and investing in completely different infrastructures that holistically support the safety and well-being of everyone. These infrastructures range from community-based accountability systems and mediation services to public safety nets like affordable and quality housing, health care, education, and public services. Thus, police abolition extends beyond simple one-to-one alternatives to policing. It encompasses methods to transform the conditions in which violence takes place and to decriminalize acts deemed as criminal in our social order. As abolitionist geographer Ruth Wilson Gilmore (Forthcoming) puts it: "Abolition requires that we change one thing: everything."

The groundswell of support for police abolition is indebted to established abolitionist activism, scholarship, and everyday living. Increasingly popular visions of abolition are rooted in the work of organizing collectives like Critical Resistance; INCITE! Women, Gender Non-Conforming, and Trans people of Color Against Violence; Black Youth Project 100; and Black Lives Matter. In addition, critical scholars such as Lindsey Dillon and Julie Sze (2016), Ruth Wilson Gilmore (2017, 2022), Alex Vitale (2017), Amna Akbar (2018), and Geo Maher (2021) contribute evidence and arguments for police-free futures in their work. Police abolition is also practiced by everyday people who replace policing with care and accountability in their daily lives.

How to Lose the Hounds has centered maroon geographies in Montgomery County, Maryland, as central models for the everyday Black life of abolition. Emerging in opposition to the policing efforts of slave catchers, a multigenerational practice of marronage in the county's historically Black communities shows how to maintain resistance to—and safety beyond—police. The folklore passed down by residents operates as a technology of escape, conveying important local knowledge for how to sustain Black life and freedom via ongoing fugitivity from violent state authority. Alongside this folklore, centuries-long spatial practices of escape from policing demonstrate the capacity of Black flight to produce lasting fugitive infrastructures that respond to and disrupt evolving dominant power structures and the police violence mobilized to maintain them. In place of policing, maroon justice centers community-based forms of accountability and structural solutions to conflict and harm. Maroon justice also models how to disrupt constructions of human value based on legal innocence. In addition to these homegrown alternatives to the criminal legal system, residents have begun reworking their relationships with the state beyond policing. Their radical praxis of community evidences ways to replace policing and the threat of police violence as an everyday tool of social control. These characteristics are not unique to historically Black communities in Montgomery County but are emblematic of abolitionist praxes made concrete across distinct but interconnected maroon geographies.

The ongoing, expansive, and radical geography of marronage offers a critical counterpoint to the institution of policing. While the social and political ramifications of slavery-era policing continuously structure our present world order, Black freedom tactics have also endured to persistently disrupt that order. As Christina Sharpe (2016, 9) reminds us: "In the wake, the past that is not past reappears, always, to rupture the present." Despite the seeming invincibility of policing, maroon geographies demonstrate that community safety and security are already operating outside of policing. This final chapter draws lessons from maroon geographies for abolition policy: plans and actions undertaken to produce a world without police.

Polic(e)(y)

The words *police* and *policy* share the same origin story. The name for *police* and the root for *policy* both originated from the classical Greek term *politeia*, which denoted all administrative matters pertaining to the city-state (Emsley 2021, 2). In ancient Athens, a number of policing functions were carried out by so-called Scythian Archers, enslaved city residents called on by public officials to maintain order and administer punishment. Their work, however, was subsumed under the totality of state functions. Likewise, early German, British, and French histories contain variants of the word *police* to refer to civil government instead of making specific reference to what we now understand as policing (Emsley 2021): "In early usage [in sixteenth-century Europe], police was indistinguishable from policy: it meant, simply, that which the state did. Whatever the state did. This genealogy reveals the tight but underrecognized relationship between police and state. Today, the uniformed [people] we call police are still doing the most basic function of the state: the monopolization of legitimate violence" (Seigel 2020). It was not until March 15, 1667, when Louis XIV named a senior official as "the *lieutenant général de police de Paris*," that the word *police* came to "refer to an institution or to those individuals charged with establishing or maintaining order, dealing with crime, and enforcing regulations" (Emsley 2021, 3). From then on, other European states began to establish police as a distinct public arm. While modern police in the United States operate in the shadow of slave patrols, they also descend from this longer history of state formation and policing.

The taut linkage between police and policy across centuries of Western history can make it challenging to imagine present policymaking aimed at police abolition. In his book envisioning a world without police, political theorist and organizer Geo Maher (2021, 136) definitively proclaimed: "Abolition is not a policy platform." While the work to achieve abolition is certainly not merely a policy matter, the transformation of laws carries the power to help make abolitionist visions more concrete. For abolition policy to meet the goals of abolition, it must be grounded in social movements and everyday places like maroon geographies where the center of policing does not hold.

The co-optation of abolitionist demands by reformists indicates the limitations of abolition policy unmoored from the larger movement for building a world without police. As calls in 2020 to abolish and defund the police rang out on a scale unseen before, several scholars reassured the public that defunding or abolishing the police did not mean entirely defunding or abolishing the police. For example, Christy E. Lopez (2020), a professor at Georgetown Law School and codirector of the school's Innovative Policing Program, wrote in the *Washington Post*: "Be not afraid. 'Defunding the police' is not as scary (or even as radical) as it sounds." Further, Lopez argued that most proponents of defunding the police simply imagine reducing police budgets and limiting the scope of police responsibilities rather than zeroing out police budgets and shutting down police departments overnight—or even at all. Amid a growing movement to defund the police, such arguments for reform have largely shaped public imaginaries, while police abolition has remained impossible for many to understand as a concept and horizon for the future.

Ironically, many reforms suggested alongside watered-down explanations for defunding the police also implicitly pave the way for further investments in policing. Reforms like civilian oversight boards, increased police force diversity, police–community collaborations, and use-of-force continuums require public money for additional training and other resources. Moreover, while such reforms have consistently failed to reduce police violence, they have been recycled time and time again, appearing on commission and task force reports ranging from the 1968 Kerner Commission Report to Obama's Task Force on 21st Century Policing. The Presidential Commission on Law Enforcement and the Administration of Justice, created by a Donald Trump executive order in 2019, was similarly tasked with making recommendations regarding police–community relations, police officer recruitment and training, and best practices for law enforcement. Subsequently, in response to Breonna Taylor's and George Floyd's fatal interactions with police, President Joe Biden issued an executive order in

2020 to increase investments in community policing to enhance trust in police within Black and Brown communities and other communities of color. These reform efforts from both sides of the institutionalized political spectrum reinforce the centrality of police instead of increasing safety and well-being.

Even some organizers whose struggles ostensibly reach toward the horizon of police abolition have limited their immediate policy recommendations to reforms aimed at making police more effective in the short term. For example, Campaign Zero's (n.d.) #8CantWait campaign in 2020 gave lip service to abolition but focused on reforms already proven to fail at reducing police violence, such as requirements for warning before shooting, a use-of-force continuum, and comprehensive reporting. In response to objections from abolitionist organizers, Campaign Zero cofounder Brittany Packnett Cunningham and data scientist Samuel Sinyangwe apologized for detracting from demands for more far-reaching solutions to police brutality.

In Minneapolis, Minnesota, where the city council famously pledged to defund the police and develop alternative public safety systems in the wake of George Floyd's murder in 2020, a police-free future for the city remains elusive. In November 2021, 56 percent of Minneapolis voters rejected a ballot measure to replace the city's police department with a public health–oriented "Department of Public Safety." Voters who did support the measure were concentrated in the areas surrounding the University of Minnesota and the neighborhood where George Floyd was killed (Oide and Van Oot 2021). The measure would have removed the police department and its chief from the city charter and eliminated the minimum funding requirement for the police force. Even if this measure succeeded, however, it still maintained the city's ability to employ police officers as part of the new public safety department.

The persistent failure of police reform demonstrates that the state cannot make amends or correct for police brutality when that very violence is foundational to ongoing state structures. In a context of systematic anti-Black state and state-sanctioned violence both within and beyond the function of police, then, how can Black justice organizing hold the state accountable via "the enforcement of public policy as a form of remediation" (Wright 2018, 5)? Moreover, if the very idea of police undergirds the meanings of policy and state activity, how can policy be retooled to build a world without police? Addressing these questions requires a radical rupture from the current terrain of policymaking. While police are integral to the foundation and endurance of the carceral state, reimagining the state beyond carcerality is possible. This imagination work creates promising opportunities for abolitionist policymaking.

Policy from Abolition Democracy to Abolition Geography

The history of Black abolitionist organizing and placemaking in the United States provides insights into the possibilities of state accountability and policy beyond investments in existing state formations. In his seminal study *Black Reconstruction in America* ([1935] 1998), W. E. B. Du Bois coins the term *abolition democracy* to describe the work of Black people following slavery's abolition in 1865 to build a new state based not only on the absence of slavery but also on equal civil rights, economic opportunity, education, and land redistribution. In this way, Black people directly worked to displace the prevailing state system rooted in their bondage. Drawing connections between Du Bois's work and prison abolition, Angela Y. Davis (2011, 73) points to "abolition democracy" as a process of "not only, or not even primarily . . . tearing down, but . . . also about building up, about creating new institutions" that would diminish the social problems that enabled and justified the very emergence of prisons. Thus, abolition democracy leaves room for reimagining and rebuilding a state beyond its current violence and limitations. A type of policymaking rooted in abolition democracy would displace the historical and ongoing use of policy as an instrument of racial, economic, gender, and sexual violence.

Abolitionist policymaking would further build upon what Ruth Wilson Gilmore (2018) terms abolition geography: the already extant "fragments and pieces, experiments and possibilities" of our future world. Through historical practices of marronage during slavery and Reconstruction-era organizing, abolition geography emerged from Black people's work to "quite literally . . . change places: to destroy the geography of slavery by mixing their labor with the external world to change the world and thereby themselves" (Gilmore 2017, 231). Today, a policy of abolition must continue this work of changing dominant geographies and the social arrangements they sustain. If *abolition democracy* entails "the creation of an array of social institutions that would begin to solve the social problems" (Davis 2011, 96), first undergirding slavery and now upholding policing and incarceration, and *abolition geography* encompasses the existing spatial experiments of such a future world, then *abolition policy* serves to solidify and extend the social solutions informing abolition democracy and materializing in abolition geography.

Abolition policy is a framework that rejects existing oppressive state formations while recognizing the supportive possibilities of the state as a site and scale of "socialized wealth and power" (Gilmore 2007, 260). Stopping short of the anarchist approach of completely denouncing the state form as inherently violent, abolition policy does reject the state's carceral powers. While current state structures inequitably distribute wealth and power by using and reproducing a monopoly on violence, abolition policy renovates state capacities according to freedom's terms. This involves a radical alternative to dismantled "welfare-warfare" structures such as Franklin D. Roosevelt's 1930s New Deal programs that unevenly distributed wealth (produced through militarism) according to race, gender, and other axes of power (Gilmore 2007, 37). It also diverges from ongoing state welfare programs, which operate through control and surveillance of potential and existing welfare recipients. Instead, abolition policy aims to uproot state violence by reducing investments in policing and incarceration and increasing investments in social goods and services.

The work of organizers committed to police-free and cage-free futures forms a critical guide for abolition policy. Policymaking grounded in the imperative of abolition must negate what abolitionists call "reformist reform," which sustains or expands the reach of police and criminal punishment rather than chipping away and reducing its overall impact (Critical Resistance 2020). To help clarify the distinction between reformist reform and steps toward police abolition, Critical Resistance (2020) lays out four central questions to ask of policy changes:

Does this . . .
> (1) Reduce funding to police?
> (2) Challenge the notion that police increase safety?
> (3) Reduce tools, tactics, and technology police have at their disposal?
> (4) Reduce the scale of policing?

If a proposed reform generates a "no" answer to these questions, it is a reformist reform. Examples include body cameras, additional training, and community policing initiatives. If a proposed step results in "yes" answers to all of the above questions, it sits along the path to abolition. Examples of abolitionist steps include suspending paid leave for cops under investigation, withdrawing participation from police militarization programs, reducing the size of police forces, and decreasing funding for police in order to prioritize public spending on community health, education, and affordable housing (Critical Resistance 2020).

Complementing Critical Resistance's delineation of the difference between reformist reforms and abolitionist changes, the Movement for Black Lives (M4BL) 2020 policy platform offers examples for a policy agenda rooted in abolitionist goals. The M4BL 2020 policy platform, "collaboratively sourced" and produced within an "ecosystem of over 170 Black-led organizations," demonstrates how policy can reduce and eliminate investments in policing while increasing commitments to life-sustaining infrastructures (M4BL 2020b, 2). The platform encompasses demands for ending the surveillance, policing, criminalization, incarceration, and deportation of Black people; closing all jails, prisons, and immigration detention centers; and investing in community-based transformative violence prevention and intervention strategies. It also puts forth demands for living-wage employment and universal, quality, and accessible health care, housing, public transportation, and education.

In contrast to "realist" policy solutions that achieve dominance by narrowing structural issues to thin, manageable problems whose resolutions necessarily fall short of transformative shifts (Gilmore 2015), the M4BL policy platform expresses a far-reaching vision for ending state and state-sanctioned violence. It outlines a Black liberation project that includes eradicating intersectional oppressions along lines of gender, sexuality, citizenship status, and criminal status. It also positions the end of policing as part of a capacious transformation of governance and an equitable restructuring of resources. As Amna A. Akbar (2018, 432) contends, the Movement for Black Lives "aims for something much broader than police reform: Black freedom, liberation, and self-determination. Indeed, the demands echo past movements, rooting the Movement's vision in a long tradition of Black radical thought and Black freedom struggles."

What Critical Resistance and the Movement for Black Lives make clear is that abolitionist policymaking requires simultaneously precise and expansive departures from the criminal legal system's laws and procedures. Abolition policy must precisely negate existing state structures and the reformist reforms that serve to apparently refine and thus sustain state violence. In unraveling state violence, abolition policy must also mobilize and expand the state's own infrastructures to support the new institutions and safety nets needed for a police-free and cage-free world. Despite ongoing and seemingly inextricable entanglements between policy and police, abolition policy offers a paradoxical way forward.

In line with the abolitionist organizing discussed earlier, maroon geographies are animated by daily practices of safety and liberation that can be rescaled to inform abolition policy. The routine life beyond policing in Montgomery County's maroon geographies demonstrates how to move toward police abolition by transforming the contexts and terms of engagement with state actors and structures. While maroon geographies do not hold all the answers, they provide expansive approaches to community well-being that challenge systems of state violence and retool state resources when possible. In this section, I outline six lessons that maroon geographies offer for abolition policy.

The first lesson centers on flight from policing. Underlying the formation of maroon geographies, the practice of flight draws attention to how apparatuses of police are escapable. Police departments, government officials, and media outlets operate together to reinforce the legitimacy of policing and an acceptance by the governed that police are indispensable to public safety and security (Hall et al. 1978). Flight from policing—in both the direct sense of the phrase and a broader sense of placemaking beyond police violence—demonstrates that, for many, safety is made possible through evading and challenging policing. In particular, people who inhabit and shape marginalized communities indicate that police actually threaten their well-being. In fact, communities of color and immigrant communities "already hesitate to call the police for fear of violence, brutality, arrest, and deportation" (Akbar 2018, 471). Instead, nonpolice systems of safety and security underscoring the practice of flight in maroon geographies enable residents to protect their lives and communities.

A large-scale, systematic practice of flight from policing might comprise harm response teams that replace police officers when threats to safety occur. Teams can be organized on a community level like the phone lines of Lincoln Park and Ken-Gar residents or institutionalized at the urban or regional scale like the Black-led nonpolice crisis response team MH First, a project of the Anti Police-Terror Project based in Oakland and Sacramento, California, which offers a free hotline that provides support on weekend nights for psychiatric crises, substance use emergencies, and domestic violence safety planning (Anti Police-Terror Project, n.d.). Abolition policy can support these grassroots civilian interventions for safety and well-being as well as retool existing public safety and security resources. For example, city-funded nonpolice crisis response teams in Eugene, Oregon, are dispatched through the police-fire-ambulance communications center. When calls are received at the 911 call center, operators dispatch unarmed mental health crisis workers and emergency medical responders if they deem that police intervention is unnecessary. This free, 24/7 mobile crisis intervention service, called CAHOOTS (Crisis Assistance Helping Out On The Streets), was organized in 1989 by the White Bird Clinic. By 2019, more than 50 percent of all 911 calls usually referred to the Eugene Police Department were handled by CAHOOTS, and many residents called CAHOOTS directly instead of 911 (Zielinski 2019). While CAHOOTS is a white-led initiative in a primarily white metropolitan area, it is an important public investment in alternatives to police. Public resources allocated to Black initiatives, such as MH First and more informal Black neighborhood networks, can further supplant police as first responders and help prevent arrests and police brutalization of people dealing with crises.

Second, as not only a form of flight but also a project of placemaking, maroon geographies evidence the need for earth-bending efforts to abolish carceral geographies. The environmental transformations required for abolition are almost already written into the landscape. During the abolitionist movement against slavery, the trees, overgrowth, swamplands, and other difficult terrains beyond the organized landscape of slavery facilitated Black flight and hidden Black geographies of freedom. Across later generations, maroon geographies were maintained by ongoing practices such as communal gardening and collective approaches to land ownership, which centered care for the earth as a vital element of building communities beyond state and state-sanctioned racism. Today, the environmental catastrophes tied to policing invite us to consider how we might organize our world differently in the path to abolition. Policing and environmental pollution work in tandem in Black and other marginalized communities to bolster uneven development. Heavily policed communities must contend with concentrations of environmental contamination ranging from Superfund sites, highways, and waste treatment facilities to the noise, light, and air pollution wrought by policing itself (Dillon and Sze 2016; Costley 2020). Abolition policy should address existing—and protect against future—environmental degradation as a project of world building beyond police. Past and ongoing movements against the interlinked harms of prisons, police, and environmental pollution model ways to understand abolition as an environmental justice struggle (Braz and Gilmore 2006; Story and Prins 2019; Narrative Arts, n.d.). Abolition policy for the twenty-first century should ensure that policies protecting our ecological future, such as those proposed under the Green New Deal (Ocasio-Cortez 2019), also protect against the endurance of carceral geographies.[1]

In the work to build a new world, abolition policy must also extricate carceral logics from planning and design, as the case of Tobytown residents' struggles against urban renewal in their neighborhood demonstrates. Dominant practices of planning and development reinforce the place of police in society: "The property relation organizes the strategy of the police state, while disinvestment and dispossession condition the production of carceral space" (Story 2019, 49). In practice, this looks like criminalizing predominately poor people of color in efforts to protect property values, to justify flows of capital out of neighborhoods labeled as dangerous, and to prime these same places to receive investment following the displacement of former residents. In defiance of this property relation, maroon geographies forward visions and practices of geographic transformations that displace police as ostensibly necessary and useful in society. In creating room for "new social relations based on economic redistribution, environmental sustainability, and the full realization of basic human and cultural rights" (Woods 1998, 2–4), Black radical vernacular development projects ranging from the Mississippi Delta region (Woods 1998) to Montgomery County, Maryland, leave no room for policing.

Third, maroon geographies also demonstrate that police abolition must be embedded in a broader program of political-economic restructuring. Creating a police-free world requires tearing down structures of racial capitalism that have undergirded the global economy since slavery. Homegrown forms of mutual aid, education and employment initiatives, and a general sense of care and collectivity shaping historically Black communities in Montgomery County echo cooperative living arrangements that enabled the formation and endurance of slavery-era maroon geographies. Even as certain cooperative arrangements have come to an end or have significantly transformed in maroon geographies, marronage continues to be a useful frame for understanding the possibilities of placemaking beyond racial capitalism. The ongoing abandonment of Black communities by government and private capital necessitates that Black people organize cooperative, noncapitalist geographic and social arrangements—albeit often entangled with practices of land ownership, wage labor, and other activities that do not allow for complete extrication from racial capitalism. Maroon geographies provide a framework for interrogating this ongoing abandonment and entanglement while simultaneously emphasizing the social worlds that Black people craft within it.

These noncapitalist engagements are an integral part of abolition since they demonstrate how to practice care and meet needs without criminalizing that need. This is especially critical as social services are increasingly tied into systems of policing and punishment. Abolition policy must eliminate control and surveillance as a precondition for access to social services. It must also address structural conditions resulting from political-economic crises such as housing insecurity, joblessness, and poverty, currently cast as individual problems to be criminalized and punished.

Fourth, maroon geographies model a transformative justice rooted in an understanding of the inextricable link between racial freedom and alternative justice approaches. Because state-sanctioned innocence has never been a place where Black people can find permanent or often even ephemeral refuge, a praxis of maroon justice has endured in Black geographies. Maroon justice is a model for community-based accountability, the valuing of all people involved in conflict or harm, and the organization of structural solutions to conflict and violence. Through maroon justice, Black community members in Montgomery County foster community accountability without solely relying on the legal constriction of the right to life and freedom. In addition to accountability measures, structural solutions enable them to address and prevent harm through investments in human needs. Regardless of the determination of a person's innocence or guilt by the state, maroon geographies show us that the imperatives for freedom and community must hold stronger than the punitive alternatives of policing and incarceration.

The scaling up of existing alternative justice practices could catalyze a transformation in dominant understandings of accountability, human value, and solutions to harm. Instead of locking up people who commit violence, what might it look like to create spaces of encounter, healing, and responsibility? How might freedom and the specter of its absence in captivity be discharged as an ideal of justice? How can building cooperative communities and addressing structural inequities diminish harm and criminalized behaviors before they occur? From Sugarland's church-based justice system to Ken-Gar residents' response to a murder committed by a community member in 1972, maroon geographies in Montgomery County demonstrate how to hold people accountable for harm while simultaneously treating harm reduction as a matter of community responsibility rather than individual choice or retribution. These maroon justice practices diverge from reformist so-called alternatives to incarceration such as neighborhood-based youth and drug courts that wrap ongoing state control and surveillance of poor Black and Brown people in the rhetoric of community, thereby producing a *"remade carceral state via the material of its own critique"* (Story 2019, 74). In recognition of the vital social ties that undergird transformative justice, abolition policy should include initiatives that maintain and expand mediation and support services that are community-driven and not embedded in the criminal legal system.

Fifth, in addition to transformative justice systems, formal mechanisms for establishing radical, participatory governance should be a part of a police abolition project rooted in maroon geographies. As Neil Roberts (2015) contends, reordering the state of society is a key element of marronage, one that involves dismantling hierarchies that order the sphere of state governance. A major facilitator of this restructuring of governance is participatory budgeting, a modern term to describe a long-term vision of Black and other marginalized communities for "fundamentally transforming the relationship among state, market, and society" (Akbar 2018, 408). By bringing together traditionally excluded people to plan an equitable allocation of municipal and public budgets, participatory budgeting can be a radically democratic process of deliberation and decision-making—the type of "abolition democracy" illuminated by Du Bois nearly a century ago.

Maroon geographies model how participatory budgeting can allow for investments in communities and human life that ultimately ensure safety more effectively than police. Lincoln Park residents' efforts to convert a police substation into an education space in 2012 demonstrate how to rework state resources and shift them away from policing. Beyond Lincoln Park, countless police stations, substations, and other carceral facilities could be transformed into similar spaces that support community education, health, and general well-being. While existing investments in community-based police infrastructure and programming support the entrenchment of state violence in communities, financial support for noncarceral community programming, organizations, and social services contributes to upending the asymmetries that foster violence and insecurity in the first place. The value of this transformation of police infrastructure becomes even more apparent when considering that police do not actually keep people safe. Police rarely apprehend people in the act of committing violence, often reacting to serious crimes *after* they occur by taking witness statements, gathering available evidence, and filing reports (Vitale 2017, 31). Aside from filing reports, the daily work of a police officer mainly involves patrolling streets, issuing tickets for parking and traffic violations, responding to noise complaints, and making misdemeanor arrests for drug possession and public "disorder" offenses like drinking in public (Vitale 2017, 31). Alternative investments in harm response teams, transformative justice, and radically participatory governance structures will help shape a more livable world for everyone.

Finally, maroon geographies demonstrate that abolition is a process of freedom struggles, not an immediate emancipation. Just as Montgomery County, Maryland, and other spaces of marronage historically served as a "liminal and transitional social space *between* slavery and freedom" (N. Roberts 2015, 4), modern-day local maroon geographies are intermediary spaces between the police state and a world with no police. While residents still must contend with police violence and at times cooperate with police, their participation often disrupts the role and logic of policing. In this way, they create openings for imagining public safety and security beyond state violence and demonstrate that police power can be contested from below. On the road to police abolition, maroon geographies structure pathways and spaces of freedom that, over time, will bring about a world without police.

Within this liminal space, maroon geographies also demonstrate how to meet human needs before and on the journey to abolition, not simply once freedom is reached. Maroon geographies evidence a thriving tradition of "Black life-making" (Mustaffa 2017, 712) in a world that has remained anti-Black since slavery. Abolition policy requires centering this geographic tradition and deprioritizing existing forms of state engagement based on reformist policies and democratic charades like civilian oversight boards. Instead of tinkering with and seeking to improve policing, Black struggles for safety and security in maroon geographies demand an attentiveness to investments in Blackness and humanity in all spheres of life. By taking seriously long-standing Black epistemologies and places of safety and security that structure these liminal geographies, we can develop grounded methods toward the eventual abolition of police.

In creating their own enclaves of Black liberation, residents of Black communities in Montgomery County and across the globe model how losing the hounds must be part of a larger project of producing geographies free from violence along lines of race, class, gender, sexuality, and other axes of power. While *How to Lose the Hounds* centers the United States in order to expand limited scholarly and popular understandings of marronage in North America, I conclude by pointing to possibilities for a global movement for police abolition. Policing is organized and conducted on a global scale; therefore, struggles against and placemaking beyond policing must also be global.

Throughout the world, police apparatuses operate in similar and interconnected ways, controlling, surveilling, and implementing violence on Black people and other colonized and formerly enslaved people. In Brazil, for example, the militarization of police to combat drugs beginning in the 1980s was partly a consequence of the Brazilian government's adaptation to and acceptance of a US-led, hemispheric "war on drugs" that targeted drug trafficking as a threat to international stability (Rodrigues 2015). Moreover, like modern reverberations of slavery-era policing in the United States, the Brazilian government's use of the military for domestic social control in primarily low-income, Black areas identified as drug zones echoes the military conquest of Indigenous and African people to facilitate colonization and slavery in Brazil. Even where there is Black governance, policing continues the violence of slavery. A case in point is Jamaica, where the most frequent victims of police brutality are poor, young Black people subjected to overcrowded and unsanitary police lock-ups, beatings, burns, and mock and actual executions (Amnesty International 2001). In Brazil, Jamaica, and across the Americas, racism remains essential to the institution of policing.

In addition, the exchange of US police practices with countries around the world extends the legacies of slavery-era policing beyond the Americas. As part of its anticommunism efforts during the Cold War, the US government helped expand police capacities in African, Asian, and Latin American countries (Schrader 2019). The International Police Academy—operated by the US Agency for International Development between 1963 and 1974—trained police officers from seventy-seven countries to prevent, contain, and suppress organizing for political and economic justice, which was condemned as communist insurgency and subversion (Marenin 1998). This training program echoed the central goal of policing to prevent "rebellion, self-emancipation, and even basic Black sociality" during chattel slavery in the United States (Schrader 2019, 34). In more recent decades, broken-windows policing—established in New York City under former two-term police commissioner William Bratton (1994–96 and 2014–16)—has been adapted in cities worldwide, including Ferguson, Los Angeles, Baltimore, London, Bangkok, San Juan, and San Salvador. Across these urban spaces, broken-windows policing echoes the way nineteenth-century US Black Codes "conflated the racialized poor with spatialized disorder" through the surveillance and punishment of poor people of color for "quality of life" offenses such as loitering and public drinking (Camp and

Heatherton 2016, 16). The export of US domestic counterinsurgency and broken-windows policing is paralleled by police departments in the United States importing inspiration and recruiting officers from US occupations in the Philippines, Haiti, Nicaragua, and other sites of colonization (Maher 2021). The modern global police regime thus reverberates with racial logics underpinning histories of both slavery and colonialism.

Just as police across the globe inherited a violent system of control and surveillance rooted in slavery and colonialism, political organizers and everyday people are heirs to tools for challenging that system and crafting radical alternatives to it. Past and ongoing marronage is foundational to such global abolitionist praxes. While formed through Black people's efforts to insulate themselves from racial violence, maroon geographies simultaneously occur within a global scalar politics enacted in response to the worldwide reach of slavery and its impacts. In this way, the impulse of isolationism undergirding marronage contributes to rather than limits radical internationalism.

Instead of struggling to abstractly envision a world without police, we can look to maroon geographies for existing and continuously emergent lessons for a global program of police abolition. The point here is not to replicate abolitionist praxes across geographic contexts in an effort to scale up but to render legible and buildable the already extant fugitive infrastructures that tie maroon geographies together. This work involves what Katherine McKittrick (2021, 6), following VèVè Clark (1990), describes as "diasporic literacy," a reading method that illuminates and connects existing diasporic practices not through endless explanation and unpacking but through "imagination and memory and study." A global abolition project rooted in maroon geographies carries the possibilities of Black diaspora geography, a "practice of recognizing black life and livingness" that demonstrates "where liberation is and might be" (McKittrick 2021, 182). While conventional mapping practices might miss the interconnectedness of Black diasporic struggles as a consequence of efforts to painstakingly chart historical and geographic continuity, Black diaspora geography draws uncommon connections across global practices of Black life and organizing. In this concluding section, I outline diasporic sites of marronage to inspire ongoing imagination work for recalling and understanding Black struggles against policing on a global scale.

Early maroon geographies serve as a scaffolding to understand Black placemaking beyond police as part of a shared, Black diasporic practice. With significant roots in the Haitian Revolution (1791–1804) and animating maroon geographies across continents, the slavery-era "political imaginary [of Black freedom] mirrored the global scope of the slave trade" (Fischer 2004, 1). In the eighteenth-century colonial Caribbean, a vibrant maroon geography connected marronage in Saint-Domingue—the home of the Haitian Revolution—with Black antislavery struggles in other colonies throughout the region. A regional communication network, or "common wind" (J. S. Scott 2020), supported this geography by circulating rumors and revolutionary impulses among maroons, sailors, free people of color, military deserters, smugglers, and people who escaped from incarceration.

Central to this network of "masterless" people (J. S. Scott 2020) was a systematic rejection of policing. In Cap-Français, Saint-Domingue—an important port city of maroon activity—enslaved people, business owners, and even authorities ignored municipal ordinances limiting the prevalence, opening hours, and liquor sales of bars, cabarets, and gambling houses. Business owners also refused to remove enslaved people from their premises (J. S. Scott 2020). More generally, since they were considered another person's property, maroons throughout the Americas committed the "crimes" of theft and rebellion against their enslavers by fleeing from slavery. Enslaved Black people also directly pushed back against policing by evading and tricking patrollers and occasionally physically retaliating against slave patrols. For example, at the start of insurrections, enslaved people in the US South routinely started fires to provide a cover for gathering at a central location (Hadden 2001). These quotidian refusals of law and policing set the material context for widespread revolution in the Americas.

Forming a counter to enduring systems of racial violence upheld and comprised by policing, Black geographies across the world are animated by many modern practices of abolition directly tied to the lineage of marronage. In the town of Accompong in western Jamaica, where maroons gained partial independence in 1739, there were no police until a police post was established in 2017. The town, known as "the safest place in the country," primarily maintains safety through community governance. Likewise, San Basilio de Palenque in Colombia, where the earliest residents secured their independence from slavery in 1603, has no police and is known for having no major crime. With the exception of extreme emergencies and in specially permitted circumstances, Colombian police cannot enter San Basilio de Palenque. Groups of residents manage community matters, and the Cimarrona Guard (La Guardia Cimarrona) protects the community from outside threats through dialogue and conflict resolution. In addition, quilombos—maroon communities in Brazil—contest state authority in their everyday lives. In the quilombo Rio dos Macacos located in the Bay of Aratu in Bahia, for example, residents ensure their safety through non-state, community-based measures despite local military police entrenchment (Bledsoe 2016). These ongoing geographies of marronage show how Black practices of safety and security that developed to structure liberation from slavery have been maintained and retooled to support ongoing freedom from state violence.

Moreover, residents of heavily policed Black urban spaces—seemingly impossible sites of police abolition—illuminate everyday pathways toward a world without police. For example, Black organizers working with the 4Front Project in London have established youth-led, community-based transformative justice practices to process and heal from harm while combating the violence of the UK criminal legal system. Likewise, the Black-led Anti Police-Terror Project based in Sacramento and Oakland works to fight policing using nonpolice responses to domestic violence, substance use, and mental health emergencies. The everyday Black life of abolition in cities also encompasses the formation of nonpolice spaces that foster Black joy and healing. In Minneapolis and Washington, DC, for example, Black Joy Sundays hosted by the Minneapolis-based Black Visions Collective and Black Lives Matter DC routinely transformed public parks into safe and affirming spaces provisionally dedicated to Black people as part of national organizing against police brutality. These Black spaces that fulfill human needs in urban centers of policing form workable openings toward the ultimate goal of police abolition.

The North American prison abolition movement also exemplifies the endurance of the historical memory of marronage in Black struggles around the criminal legal system. For example, political prisoner Russell "Maroon" Shoatz—nicknamed as such following a twenty-seven-day escape from the state prison in Huntingdon, Pennsylvania, in 1977—embodies a maroon consciousness that characterized revolutionaries at the vanguard of the 1970s US Black liberation movement. Shoatz (2013) himself urged organizers to build upon the legacies of marronage in struggles against mass incarceration, specifically, and capitalism and patriarchy more broadly. Likewise, Black transgender and gender-nonconforming prison abolitionists in the United States and Canada draw on the legacy of "maroon insurgencies" in their activism by identifying contemporary state surveillance, policing, and incarceration as sites of "sexual-racial terror" that continue from the institution of slavery to sustain the "current mode of capitalist exploitation" (Oparah 2015, 335). Like their maroon predecessors—who called on supernatural powers derived from African spirituality and united with Indigenous and white people exiled from the slave economy—these abolitionist activists build out multiracial coalitions and incorporate Indigenous and African diasporic spiritual and alterative justice practices in their work to shift antiprison organizing beyond the gender binary.

Black geographies across the globe demonstrate that abolishing prisons and police is not just possible but also already has roots in existing practices of community building, care, and accountability that refuse, disrupt, and elude state violence. The lineage of abolition extending from the era of slavery continues to shape daily Black life and placemaking globally as well as cross-racial, radical organizing beyond policing and incarceration. Contemporary and future scholar-activism and movement building can draw from these models of ongoing maroon organizing in Jamaica, Colombia, Brazil, Canada, the United States, and beyond to facilitate a shared, diasporic practice of world building beyond state violence. In the current reckoning with the violent past and impossible future of criminal punishment, we must attend to and extend global Black abolitionist praxes to create a world free of police and cages.

Maroon geographies also offer an open-ended blueprint for a world-building project beyond racial violence more generally. While this book focuses on struggles with and alternatives to policing, Black freedom practices rooted in flight from slavery underscore the development and organization of Black visions of justice in housing, education, health care, and other human needs. Examining Black abolitionist praxes through the historical and ongoing geography of marronage demonstrates that the end of policing is interlinked with these larger transformations. More broadly, the framework of maroon geographies fosters possibilities for linking scholarship and organizing around legacies of "colonialism, slavery, capitalism, and empire" that intimately intertwine Europe, Africa, Asia, and the Americas (Lowe 2015, 2). In the context of globally oriented political organizing, the Danish collective Marronage exemplifies such scalar possibilities of maroon geographies. Marronage is a collective of Black feminists and other people of color based in Copenhagen, Denmark, who draw connections between the history of marronage and present-day international countermovements against neocolonialism, racial capitalism, and patriarchy (Marronage, n.d.). The collective publishes multimedia content, including a journal called *Marronage*, and works in collaboration with other groups to organize community spaces, events, and demonstrations that center Black diasporic issues.

Marronage is an enduring, expansive, and radical geographic praxis of producing places full of care, joy, and life. Maroon geographies connect centuries-long patterns of flight from and placemaking beyond global racial capitalism and its attendant violences. It is my hope that *How to Lose the Hounds* operates like maroon folklore, as a technology of escape, by proposing how we might look to past and ongoing Black fugitivity to better understand how to create and sustain Black life and freedom in our future. The abolitionist grammar underscoring this book both emerges from and signals the unbounded possibilities of such noncarceral geographies. By no means is the story finished.

Epilogue: Abolition Future Folklore

It is a year not very far in the distant future. Police no longer exist. City budgets are allocated primarily by the votes of Black people, Indigenous people, other communities of color, working-class people, people with disabilities, and other descendants of those formerly marginalized in society. They choose to fund community centers, parks and gardens, youth recreation programs, public schools, libraries, health clinics, accessible public transportation, and housing for all. Access to these spaces is not contingent on control or surveillance. There are also jobs programs, civilian crisis response teams, and free counseling and mediation services.

As a response to waves of mass uprisings in the decades before, police departments shrunk down to nothing as their budgets were slowly turned over to these other public safety nets, which reduced—and held people accountable for—behaviors that used to be criminalized. Police forces were mandated to enact hiring freezes and eliminate overtime, and police officers lost their jobs and pensions when they brutalized other people. There is a museum exhibit in town on the half-life of police, showing how quickly the instability of policing led to its decay once people came to understand the transformative possibilities of a world beyond policing.

You live in a community that reflects the root sense of the word: common, public, shared. You don't recall a time when that wasn't the case for you or for all of those in your life's orbit. You spend your time working in a community garden and a collective neighborhood pantry. You intimately know your neighbors and share food, money, and other resources with them. This mutuality results from the abundance of resources available, not because of anyone's lack of means or of access to what they need or desire. All megacorporations were transformed into cooperatives, bringing the land, infrastructure, and tools of production to the collective ownership and governance of the people. The global networks of people and resources formerly undergirding those corporations now support an emerging world-scaled solidarity economy that meets everyone's needs without exploiting any body or place.

There are no fences, iron bars, or gates designed to keep anyone out from anywhere on the earth's surface. You remember a story that your grandmother told you about a time of such hostile architecture, inverted versions of the cages that used to keep people locked away from the rest of the world. You always shiver at the thought of justice being seemingly served behind cold metal bars. You also learned of the generations of everyday people who organized on a global scale to counteract the planet-spanning institutions of policing, criminal punishment, and militarism. You learned that this new world was formed through the visions and experiments of people like maroons to practice safety and well-being on their own terms.

The journey of collective flight from policing was complicated. It took time for the structural transformations to take root that have now diminished violence and other criminalized behaviors. Before everyone's needs were met and when people still struggled to survive, however, people began serving those needs after moments of harm or crisis. You heard that a man received a free meal and a survival grant after he tried to buy groceries and cigarettes with counterfeit money. When a young father was shot and lost his life, a community-based justice team met with the shooter and the grieving family to assess and meet their needs, facilitate an apology, and design a plan for reparations—not retribution. Two children who fought in school were able to heal through a transformative encounter mediated by a team of counselors. When someone experiencing a mental health crisis risked endangering their self or others, they were offered a treatment plan that made them feel whole. When a woman saw another woman sleeping in her car across the street from her home, she connected her to an emergency shelter and a new free housing program. Over time, news about harms faded away as flight from policing came to shape the whole world, place by place.

Now, the old police stations, jails, detention centers, and prisons are unrecognizable as carceral geographies. Many of these sites were transformed into health clinics and hospitals—once abandoned in the expansion of policing and prisons. Other sites now house green energy infrastructure like wind and solar farms. In rural former prison towns, local ecosystems are now restored after histories of extraction from harmful agricultural and mining practices and later the accumulated environmental impacts of prisons.

The world is not a utopia. There is still work to be done to unsettle power structures. But the old foundations are shaken up in a beautiful way. When it comes to police abolition, you almost cannot imagine a time when people used to ask, "What would we do without police?" The hounds are so long lost that they absolutely refuse to follow the future's tracks.

Notes

Prologue

1   The Citizens' Committee for Justice was the product of combined efforts of churches, ministers, the *Afro-American* newspaper, the NAACP, and other groups in the city of Baltimore. All quotations from Hughes and White are from the *Baltimore Afro-American* 1942.

2   Black police officers in Baltimore at the time were prevented from wearing uniforms "so as not to intimidate whites" (Baum 2010, 40).

3   Epitomizing the failures of police diversity as a solution to police violence, in 1967, the Montgomery County, Maryland, police department held a recruitment drive at local military installations to integrate its all-white police force (Rovner 1967). The siting of police recruitment on military grounds exemplifies how increased diversity does not counter police violence; in this case, the militarization of police was only further entrenched. In addition, Black police officers have not proven to be less prejudiced or less violent than white officers (Moskos 2008).

Introduction

1   Organizer Mariame Kaba, in a 2017 interview with John Duda of The Real News Network, described the suburb of Naperville, Illinois, as a place where abolition is practiced already in the absence of police and metal detectors in schools and in the presence of jobs, housing, and health care. Sociologist Alex Vitale pointed to wealthy suburban communities when asked about his vision for the future during a 2020 NPR interview with Ari Shapiro about defunding the police. He explained that residents in these communities are able to mobilize their own resources for drug treatment and mental health care as alternatives to police involvement. In a 2020 virtual town hall, Congressperson Alexandria Ocasio-Cortez argued that suburbs show us what a world where

we defund the police looks like (Dixon 2020). She contrasted suburban investments in schools and school counselors with the urban school-to-prison pipeline to explain how funding from police in cities could be shifted to improve safety for young people.

2 For a discussion of the connection between slave patrols and border patrols, see Jimenez 2000, 35.

3 The Fugitive Slave Acts of 1793 and 1850 authorized law enforcement to apprehend and return alleged runaways who escaped from one state into another state or federal territory. The 1793 law allowed judicial authorities to deny Black people a jury trial in the determination of their alleged fugitive slave status. The 1850 law also prohibited alleged fugitives from testifying on their own behalf and imposed penalties on people who helped enslaved people escape and law enforcement agents who refused to enforce the law.

4 On the argument of Ruth Wilson Gilmore's "Too Soon for Sorry," delivered as the 2016 Marion Thompson Wright Lecture at Rutgers University–Newark, see https://www.newark.rutgers.edu/news/racism-past-present-prison-policing.

5 Slavery was abolished in Maryland through the passage of the Maryland Constitution of 1864. Despite its earlier abolition of slavery, Maryland did not necessarily denounce slavery more than other southern states. For example, within Montgomery County, 76 percent of voters in the Maryland Constitutional Election of October 1864 voted against the constitution because they did not want an end to slavery in Maryland. Statewide, 52 percent of Maryland County voters voted against the constitution (Wagandt 2004). In fact, after the county votes had been tallied, the *Maryland Union* newspaper jubilantly headlined on October 20, 1864: "MARYLAND REDEEMED! THE NEGRO-ROBBING CONSTITUTION DEFEATED! DEATH KNELL OF ABOLITIONISM! MARYLAND SAFE FOR MCCLELLAN! HANG YOUR HEADS FOR SHAME—YE SCOUNDRELS!" It was not until the votes of Maryland's soldiers fighting in the US Civil War were counted that the constitution was approved. The soldiers overwhelmingly supported the new constitution, and consequently slavery was abolished in Maryland with its passage.

6 Maryland had the largest free Black population in the country between 1810 and 1865 (Fields 1985, 1). In 1860, across the state of Maryland, there were almost as many free Black people as there were enslaved: eighty-seven thousand. In fact, Maryland's large free Black population was a major grievance among Maryland enslavers, especially in light of the continuous losses of enslaved laborers who escaped from the border state (Brackett 1890).

1. Maroon Folklore as an Abolition Technology

1   In Sandy Spring, the 1777 banning of the importation, purchase, and sale of enslaved people by the Quaker Society of Friends in Maryland contributed to a growing local population of free Black people who helped fugitives from slavery (Cohen 1995). By 1815, most Black residents of Sandy Spring were free, and many of them remained in the area, settling on land that Quaker residents gave or sold to them (Fly and Fly 1983, 117). This free Black community played an important role in developing a small safe haven for maroons escaping north. Black Sandy Spring–area residents who are recorded as helping fugitives in their flight to freedom include a local blacksmith named Samuel Adams; Harriet Smallwood, who harbored runaways in her home after she was manumitted in 1840; and Enoch George Howard, a formerly enslaved man who was manumitted in 1851 (Cohen 2006). In addition to local Black residents, some of the Sandy Spring Quakers themselves are also believed to have provided clothing, food, and money to maroons (Cohen 2006). The existence of a number of hidden rooms, secret cellars, and a system of underground tunnels between Quaker residences signals the role that local Quakers played in harboring fugitives from slavery (Cohen 1994, 25–26).

2   Dance's (1987, 169n3) book contains an extensive list of words used in the Black lexicon to describe and encourage flight: "Air out, back off, backtrack, beat it, blow, breeze, brush off, bust out, cop a drill/trot, crash out, cruise, cut, cut out, cut and run, depart, disappear, dodge, drift, duck out, ease on out, ease on down, escape, fade, flake out/off, flee, fly, fly the coop, foot it, freewheel, get on in/off/down/out/back, go, go away, go North, go over the hill/wall, grab a armful of box-cars/the first thing smoking, hat up, haul ass/it, hightail it, hike, hit the road/street, hoof it, hustle, journey, jump bail, jump a train, lam (or take a lam), leave, light out, make feet help the body, make it, make oneself scarce, make tracks, ooze, percolate, ride, ride the rails, roll out/on, run, scat, scram, sell out, shove, shove off, skip, skivver, slide, space, split, step, take a powder/duck, take off, take it to the woods/hills/road, trilly on, trilly walk, trot, truck, truck it, tunnel (go into hiding), vamoose, wheel it, wing it."

3   Judah Schept (2015, 29) develops the theoretical analytic "carceral habitus" as a way to account for "the locally situated ways in which the logics and practices of hegemonic carcerality take shape, at times in contrast to its more familiar forms at the level of the state and nation." This analytic stems from Pierre Bourdieu's conceptualization of habitus as "a set of boundaries or limitations of consciousness or ability, within which an infinite number of iterations of given practices or institutions are possible, albeit constrained" (qtd. in Schept 2015, 11). The concept

"carceral habitus" helps explain how mass incarceration reproduces itself through the permutation of hegemonic logics into local political and cultural contexts.

2. The Fugitive Infrastructure of Maroon Geographies

1 An 1818 Maryland General Assembly law declared that people convicted of harboring fugitives from slavery could be confined in the penitentiary for up to six years. Samuel Davis of Montgomery County, for example, was sentenced in 1842 to five years and eight months in the Maryland Penitentiary for assisting a man named Henry in running away from his enslaver Ann Griffith (Maryland State Archives).

2 Those who heard the police radio dispatch gave conflicting accounts of which term was used to describe Twyman's race.

3 Following the completion of my archival research in 2018, archivists at Montgomery History (the county's historical society) revised the restricted records within the Human Relations Commission collection, unrestricting all files that do not relate to minors or contain records specifically marked confidential—this includes files pertaining to Twyman's case and other Human Relations Commission Justice Committee compliance complaints. I was told that my research in the collection helped bring attention to the need to revisit past archival restrictions in the Montgomery History archives and increase record accessibility to support relevant research today.

4 Simone Browne (2015) posits that sousveillance has enabled people to respond to, challenge, and confront anti-Black surveillance from the era of slavery to the present-day United States. The anti-Black tools of social control buttressing spaces as far ranging as plantations to twenty-first-century airports, Browne (2015, 21) contends, have been "appropriated, co-opted, repurposed, and challenged in order to facilitate survival and escape." She calls this particular form of sousveillance "dark sousveillance."

3. Maroon Justice

1 Even with the decline of praise houses, Gullahs used community meetings to maintain their own justice procedures. A notable example is an accidental killing of a Gullah by another community member in the early 2000s, after which the victim's family turned to a community coalition meeting as an alternative to civil court. During the meeting, community members discussed the actions and background of the per-

son responsible for the killing. This person was able to remain in the community and, as a form of reparations following the meeting, contributed a monthly basket of food to the victim's family (Jenkins 2006).

2   The use of the abbreviation SCAT! was quite fitting for a group of Scotland residents dedicated to what I am calling maroon justice because the word *scat* is a popular term for flight in the Black lexicon (Dance 1987, 169n3) and also describes a technique of vocal improvisation in jazz. Maroon justice requires both flight from existing systems of criminal law enforcement and the improvisation of something new.

4. Community beyond Policing

1   Tobytown resident Phyllis Shaw critiqued the police-involved tutoring program and pointed out that "if you can pay two cops to sit there all day, you can pay one teacher" (Wraga 2001b).

2   Seigel (2018, 19) explains that even while modern socialist and communist state regimes have rhetorically challenged the state-market, they still operate within the dominating framework of global capitalism.

5. Maroon Geographies and the Paradox of Abolition Policy

1   The Green New Deal (Ocasio-Cortez 2019) was introduced in the US House of Representatives in 2019. It called for a ten-year effort to reduce pollution and greenhouse gas emissions; expand green infrastructure and industry; invest in living-wage jobs; and provide affordable and high-quality health care, housing, and higher education to all. Many modern green criminal justice initiatives—including green prisons and low-emissions police vehicles—give lip service to sustainability goals like those delineated in the Green New Deal while ultimately staking a claim for the continued place of carceral geographies in our "greening" world. Abolition policy's counterwork against state violence should be an indispensable component of sustainability initiatives.

References

"An Act Relating to Servants and Slaves." 1676. In *Proceedings and Acts of the General Assembly of Maryland: April 1666–June 1676*, 523–28. Archives of Maryland Online. https://msa.maryland.gov/megafile/msa/speccol/sc2900/sc2908/000001/000002/pdf/am2—523.pdf.

Afro-American (Baltimore). 1942. "Cop Kills Fort Meade Soldier, 26." February 3. Page 1. The AFRO Archives (https://afro.com/archives/). https://news.google.com/newspapers?id=EZ4lAAAAIBAJ&sjid=4_QFAAAAIBAJ&pg=3240%2C438547.

Afro-American (Baltimore). 1942. "What Spokesmen Demanded at Epochal March on Annapolis." April 28. Page 2. The AFRO Archives (https://afro.com/archives/). https://news.google.com/newspapers?id=HJ4lAAAAIBAJ&sjid=4_QFAAAAIBAJ&pg=1159%2C1863668.

Afro-American Institute for Historic Preservation and Community Development. 1978. "A Study of Historic Sites in the Metropolitan Washington Regions of Northern Virginia and Southern Maryland Importantly Related to the History of Afro-Americans Part III." Lincoln Park Folder I—Year 2003. Peerless Rockville Historic Preservation Ltd., Rockville, MD.

Agorsah, Emmanuel Kofi. 1994. *Maroon Heritage: Archaeological, Ethnographic, and Historical Perspectives*. Barbados: Canoe.

Akbar, Amna A. 2018. "Toward a Radical Imagination of Law." *New York University Law Review* 93 (3): 405–79. https://doi.org/10.2139/ssrn.3061917.

Alexander, Apryl A., Hailey Allo, and Hannah Klukoff. 2020. "Sick and Shut In: Incarceration during a Public Health Crisis." *Journal of Humanistic Psychology* 60 (5): 647–56. https://doi.org/10.1177/0022167820930556.

Amnesty International. 2001. "JAMAICA: Killings and Violence by Police: How Many More Victims?" April 9. https://www.amnesty.org/en/documents/amr38/007/2001/en/.

Anderson, Jane. 1999. "Free African-Americans in Maryland: The Underground Railroad in Sandy Spring, Maryland: 1800–1860." Ladson Research Library and Archives, Sandy Spring Slave Museum and African Art Gallery, Sandy Spring, MD.

Anderson, Jean Bradley. 1990. *Durham County: A History of Durham County, North Carolina*. Durham, NC: Duke University Press.

Anti Police-Terror Project. n.d. "M.H.FIRST: Community First Response." Accessed December 6, 2021. https://www.antipoliceterrorproject.org/mental -health-first.

Aptheker, Herbert. 1939. "Maroons within the Present Limits of the United States." *Journal of Negro History* 24 (2): 167–84. https://doi.org/10.2307/2714447.

Aptheker, Herbert. 1947. "Additional Data on American Maroons." *Journal of Negro History* 32 (4): 452–60. https://doi.org/10.2307/2714927.

Baltimore City Police Department. n.d. "BPD History." Accessed March 17, 2023. https://baltimorecitypolicedept.org/citypolice/bpd-history.html#African _Americans_in_the_department.

Baltimore Sun. 1845. "Fifty Dollars Reward." June 13.

Baltimore Sun. 1859. "$100 Reward." April 30.

Baltimore Sun. 2015. "Why Freddie Gray Ran." April 26.

Baum, Howell S. 2010. *"Brown" in Baltimore: School Desegregation and the Limits of Liberalism*. Ithaca, NY: Cornell University Press.

Baxter, Leslie A., and Barbara M. Montgomery. 1996. *Relating: Dialogues and Dialectics*. New York: Guilford.

Beckett, Katherine, and Naomi Murakawa. 2012. "Mapping the Shadow Carceral State: Toward an Institutionally Capacious Approach to Punishment." *Theoretical Criminology* 16 (2): 221–44. https://doi.org/10.1177/1362480612442113.

Benjamin, Ruha, ed. 2019. *Captivating Technology: Race, Carceral Technoscience, and Liberatory Imagination in Everyday Life*. Durham, NC: Duke University Press.

Billingsley, Andrew. 2003. *Mighty like a River: The Black Church and Social Reform*. New York: Oxford University Press.

Blackmon, Douglas A. 2008. *Slavery by Another Name: The Re-Enslavement of Black Americans from the Civil War to World War II*. New York: Anchor Books.

Blankenheim, Michael. 1985. "Canada Jim—Slaves' Angel of Freedom." *Montgomery (MD) Journal*, February 1. Slavery—Sandy Spring Area folder. Jane C. Sween Research Library and Special Collections, Montgomery History, Rockville, MD.

Bledsoe, Adam. 2016. "Defender Nosso Pedaço de Chão: Quilombola Struggles in Bahia." PhD diss., University of North Carolina at Chapel Hill.

Bledsoe, Adam. 2017. "Marronage as a Past and Present Geography in the Americas." *Southeastern Geographer* 57 (1): 30–50. https://doi.org/10.1353/sgo.2017 .0004.

Bledsoe, Adam. 2021. "Neither Ground on Which to Stand, nor Self to Defend: The Structural Denial (and Radical Histories) of Black Self-Defense." *Annals of the American Association of Geographers* 112 (5): 1296–1312. https://doi.org/10 .1080/24694452.2021.1963657.

Bloch, Stefano. 2021. "Policing Car Space and the Legal Liminality of the Automobile." *Progress in Human Geography* 45 (1): 136–55. https://doi.org/10.1177 /0309132519901306.

Bonilla, Yarimar. 2015. *Non-Sovereign Futures: French Caribbean Politics in the Wake of Disenchantment*. Chicago: University of Chicago Press.

Bonner, Alice. 1974. "Tobytown: New Housing, Old Problems." *Washington Post*, July 5.

Brackett, Jeffrey R. 1890. *Notes on the Progress of the Colored People of Maryland since the War*. Baltimore: Johns Hopkins University Press.

Braithwaite, John. 2002. *Restorative Justice and Responsive Regulation*. Oxford: Oxford University Press.

Braz, Rose, and Craig Gilmore. 2006. "Joining Forces: Prisons and Environmental Justice in Recent California Organizing." *Radical History Review* 2006 (96): 95–111. https://doi.org/10.1215/01636545-2006-006.

Browne, Jaron. 2010. "Rooted in Slavery: Prison Labor Exploitation." *Race, Poverty & the Environment* 17 (1): 78–80.

Browne, Simone. 2015. *Dark Matters: On the Surveillance of Blackness*. Durham, NC: Duke University Press.

Buday, Mackenzie, and Ashley Nellis. 2022. "Private Prisons in the United States." *Sentencing Project*, August 23. https://www.sentencingproject.org/reports/private-prisons-in-the-united-states/.

Bureau of the Census. 1961. *1960 Census: Population*. Vol. 1, *Characteristics of the Population, Part 1–57*. https://www.census.gov/library/publications/1961/dec/population-vol-01.html.

Burns, Kathryn. 1992. "Ken-Gar Community Celebrates 100 Years." *Montgomery County (MD) Sentinel*, April 30. Jane C. Sween Research Library and Special Collections, Montgomery History, Rockville, MD.

Camp, Jordan T., and Christina Heatherton. 2016. "Introduction: Policing the Planet." In *Policing the Planet: Why the Policing Crisis Led to Black Lives Matter*, 12–21. London: Verso.

Campaign Zero. n.d. "#8CANTWAIT." Accessed March 26, 2021. https://8cantwait.org/.

Campbell, Stanley W. 1970. *The Slave Catchers: Enforcement of the Fugitive Slave Law, 1850-1860*. Chapel Hill: University of North Carolina Press.

Center for Popular Democracy, Law for Black Lives, and Black Youth Project 100. 2017. "Freedom to Thrive: Reimagining Safety and Security in Our Communities." https://populardemocracy.org/sites/default/files/Freedom%20To%20Thrive%2C%20Higher%20Res%20Version.pdf.

Center for Research on Criminal Justice. 1977. *The Iron Fist and the Velvet Glove: An Analysis of the U.S. Police*. 2nd ed. Berkeley, CA: Center for Research on Criminal Justice.

City of Rockville Planning Commission. 2013. *Annual Report 2012*. https://www.rockvillemd.gov/DocumentCenter/View/5107/Planning-Commission-Annual-Report-2012?bidId.

City Planning Associates, Inc. 1969. *Montgomery County Community Renewal Program Maryland R-39 (CR): Community Development Potential*. Report 8. Falls Church, VA: The Associates.

Clark, VèVè. 1990. "Developing Diaspora Literacy: Allusion in Maryse Condé's Hérémakhonon." In *Out of the Kumbla: Caribbean Women and Literature*, edited by Carole Boyce Davies and Elaine Savory Fido, 303–19. Trenton, NJ: Africa World Press.

Cohen, Anthony. 1994. *The Underground Railroad in Montgomery County, Maryland: A History and Driving Guide.* Ladson Research Library and Archives, Sandy Spring Slave Museum and African Art Gallery, Sandy Spring, MD.

Cohen, Anthony. 1995. "The Underground Railroad in Montgomery County." *Montgomery County Story* 38 (1): 321–31.

Cohen, Anthony. 2006. "The Underground Railroad in Montgomery County: Recent Finds and Revelations." *Montgomery County Story* 49 (1): 96–107.

Community Cornerstones: African American Communities in Montgomery County, Maryland. 2014. Heritage Tourism Alliance of Montgomery County, MD (Heritage Montgomery). DVD.

Costley, Drew. 2020. "Defunding the Police Is an Environmental Justice Issue." *OneZero* (blog), June 18. https://onezero.medium.com/defunding-the-police -is-an-environmental-justice-issue-9c14e48e1ce5.

Cowen, Deborah. 2017. "Infrastructures of Empire and Resistance." *Verso Books* (blog), January 25. https://www.versobooks.com/blogs/3067-infrastructures -of-empire-and-resistance.

Critical Resistance. 2020. "Reformist Reforms vs. Abolitionist Steps in Policing." May 14. https://criticalresistance.org/resources/reformist-reforms-vs -abolitionist-steps-in-policing/.

Curtis, Frances V. 1972. "An Oral History Interview with Frances Vinson Curtis (Mrs. Roger)." Civic Leader Interview by Helen Scharf. Transcript. Montgomery County Archives, Montgomery History, Gaithersburg, MD.

Dance, Daryl Cumber. 1987. *Long Gone: The Mecklenburg Six and the Theme of Escape in Black Folklore.* Knoxville: University of Tennessee Press.

Davis, Angela Y. 2003. *Are Prisons Obsolete?* New York: Seven Stories.

Davis, Angela Y. 2011. *Abolition Democracy: Beyond Empire, Prisons, and Torture.* New York: Seven Stories.

Davis, Janae, Alex A. Moulton, Levi Van Sant, and Brian Williams. 2019. "Anthropocene, Capitalocene, . . . Plantationocene? A Manifesto for Ecological Justice in an Age of Global Crises." *Geography Compass* 13 (5): e12438. https://doi .org/10.1111/gec3.12438.

Davis, Rande. 2008. "The Sweet Taste of Liberty." *Monocacy Monocle* (Montgomery and Frederick Counties, MD), April 11. Communities files—Sugarland. Jane C. Sween Research Library and Special Collections, Montgomery History, Rockville, MD.

Davis, Rande. 2015. "Sugarland Forest: A Historical Look Back." *Monocacy Monocle* (Montgomery and Frederick Counties, MD), February 13. Communities files—Sugarland. Jane C. Sween Research Library and Special Collections, Montgomery History, Rockville, MD.

Dillon, Lindsey, and Julie Sze. 2016. "Police Power and Particulate Matters: Environmental Justice and the Spatialities of In/Securities in U.S. Cities." *English Language Notes* 54 (September). https://doi.org/10.1215/00138282-54.2.13.

Diouf, Sylviane A. 2014. *Slavery's Exiles: The Story of the American Maroons*. New York: New York University Press.

Dixon, Emily. 2020. "Alexandria Ocasio-Cortez Was Asked about Defunding the Police and Her Answer Went Viral." *Marie Claire*, June 12. https://ocasio-cortez.house.gov/media/in-the-news/alexandria-ocasio-cortez-was-asked-about-defunding-police-and-her-answer-went.

Donaghue, Erin. 2008. "Scotland Students Uncover Their Community's Past." *Gazette* (Maryland), November 26. Communities files—Scotland. Jane C. Sween Research Library and Special Collections, Montgomery History, Rockville, MD.

Douglas, Walter B. 1965. "A House Is Not a Home in Toby Town: It's a Crate." *Washington Post*, November 14.

Du Bois, W. E. B. (1903) 2015. *The Souls of Black Folk*. New Haven, CT: Yale University Press.

Du Bois, W. E. B. (1935) 1998. *Black Reconstruction in America, 1860–1880*. New York: Free Press.

Duffin, Sharyn. 2001. "Lincoln Park Historic District." Communities files—Lincoln Park. Jane C. Sween Research Library and Special Collections, Montgomery History, Rockville, MD.

Eckardt, Wolf Von. 1967. "Toby Town Plan Could Solve 2 Important Problems: A Critique." *Washington Post*, October 1.

Eisman, Amy. 1977. "Lincoln Park: Black Community Keeps Its Roots in a Transient County." *Montgomery County (MD) Sentinel*, July 28. Communities files—Lincoln Park. Jane C. Sween Research Library and Special Collections, Montgomery History, Rockville, MD.

Emsley, Clive. 2021. *A Short History of Police and Policing*. Oxford: Oxford University Press.

Evening Star (Washington, DC). 1857. "Fugitive Slaves." May 11. Chronicling America: Historic American Newspapers, Library of Congress, Washington, DC. https://chroniclingamerica.loc.gov/lccn/sn83045462/1857-05-11/ed-1/seq-3/.

Ferretti, Federico. 2019. "Decolonizing the Northeast: Brazilian Subalterns, Non-European Heritages, and Radical Geography in Pernambuco." *Annals of the American Association of Geographers* 109 (5): 1632–50. https://doi.org/10.1080/24694452.2018.1554423.

Fields, Barbara Jeanne. 1985. *Slavery and Freedom on the Middle Ground: Maryland during the Nineteenth Century*. New Haven, CT: Yale University Press.

Fischer, Sibylle. 2004. *Modernity Disavowed: Haiti and the Cultures of Slavery in the Age of Revolution*. Durham, NC: Duke University Press.

Flock-Darko, Barbara. 1992. "Ken-Gar." *Montgomery (MD) Times*, November. Communities files—Ken Gar. Jane C. Sween Research Library and Special Collections, Montgomery History, Rockville, MD.

Fly, Everett L., and La Barbara Wigfall Fly. 1983. *Northeastern Montgomery County Black Oral History Study*. Rockville, MD: Entourage, Inc.

Forman, James, Jr. 2017. *Locking Up Our Own: Crime and Punishment in Black America*. New York: Farrar, Straus and Giroux.

Frazier, E. Franklin. 1974. *The Negro Church in America*. New York: Schocken Books.

Freeman, James. 2014. "Raising the Flag over Rio de Janeiro's Favelas: Citizenship and Social Control in the Olympic City." *Journal of Latin American Geography* 13 (1): 7–38. https://doi.org/10.1353/lag.2014.0016.

Gaunt, Evelyn. 1979. "Notes from Evelyn Gaunt, for Black History Exhibit 1979." Lincoln Park Folder I—Year 2003. Peerless Rockville Historic Preservation Ltd., Rockville, MD.

Gibson-Graham, J. K. 2006. *A Postcapitalist Politics*. Minneapolis: University of Minnesota Press.

Gibson-Graham, J. K., Jenny Cameron, Kelly Dombroski, Stephen Healy, Ethan Miller, and the Community Economies Collective. 2017. "Cultivating Community Economies: Tools for Building a Liveable World." August. The Next System Project. https://thenextsystem.org/sites/default/files/2017-08/JKGibsonGraham-1-1.pdf.

Gilmore, Ruth Wilson. 2007. *Golden Gulag: Prisons, Surplus, Crisis, and Opposition in Globalizing California*. Berkeley: University of California Press.

Gilmore, Ruth Wilson. 2008. "Forgotten Places and the Seeds of Grassroots Planning." In *Engaging Contradictions: Theory, Politics, and Methods of Activist Scholarship*, edited by Charles R. Hale, 31–61. Berkeley: University of California Press.

Gilmore, Ruth Wilson. 2015. "The Worrying State of the Anti-Prison Movement." *Social Justice: A Journal of Crime, Conflict and World Order* (blog), February 23. http://www.socialjusticejournal.org/the-worrying-state-of-the-anti-prison-movement/.

Gilmore, Ruth Wilson. 2016. "Too Soon for Sorry." Marion Thompson Wright Lecture, Rutgers University–Newark, February 20.

Gilmore, Ruth Wilson. 2017. "Abolition Geography and the Problem of Innocence." In *Futures of Black Radicalism*, edited by Gaye Theresa Johnson and Alex Lubin, 225–40. New York: Verso.

Gilmore, Ruth Wilson. 2018. "Making Abolition Geography in California's Central Valley." *The Funambulist*, December 20. https://thefunambulist.net/magazine/21-space-activism/interview-making-abolition-geography-california-central-valley-ruth-wilson-gilmore.

Gilmore, Ruth Wilson. 2022. *Abolition Geography: Essays towards Liberation*. New York: Verso.

Gilmore, Ruth Wilson. Forthcoming. *Change Everything: Racial Capitalism and the Case for Abolition*. Edited by Naomi Murakawa. Chicago: Haymarket Books.

Gilmore, Ruth Wilson, and Craig Gilmore. 2007. "Restating the Obvious." In *Indefensible Spaces: The Architecture of the National Security State*, edited by Michael Sorkin, 141–62. New York: Routledge.

Gilmore, Ruth Wilson, and Craig Gilmore. 2016. "Beyond Bratton." In *Policing the Planet: Why the Policing Crisis Led to Black Lives Matter*, edited by Jordan T. Camp and Christina Heatherton, 173–99. London: Verso.

Glissant, Édouard. 1999. *Caribbean Discourse: Selected Essays*. Charlottesville: University Press of Virginia.

Gordon, Avery F. 2017. "The Bruise Blues." In *Futures of Black Radicalism*, edited by Gaye Theresa Johnson and Alex Lubin, 194–205. New York: Verso.

Governor's Commission on Problems Affecting the Negro Population. 1943. "Report of the Governor's Commission on Problems Affecting the Negro Population." University of Maryland, College Park.

Green, Edward C. 1977. "Social Control in Tribal Afro-America." *Anthropological Quarterly* 50 (3): 107–16. https://doi.org/10.2307/3317590.

Gregg, Jessica J. 1990. "Lincoln Park Strives to Improve Image." *Business Record* (Montgomery County, MD), November 11. Communities files—Lincoln Park. Jane C. Sween Research Library and Special Collections, Montgomery History, Rockville, MD.

Griffin, Horace. 2000. "Their Own Received Them Not: African American Lesbians and Gays in Black Churches." *Theology and Sexuality* 2000 (12): 88–100. https://doi.org/10.1177/135583580000601206.

Gumbs, Alexis Pauline. 2015. "Evidence." In *Octavia's Brood: Science Fiction Stories from Social Justice Movements*, edited by adrienne maree brown and Walidah Imarisha, 33–41. Oakland, CA: AK Press.

Gutheim, Frederick. 1949. *The Potomac*. New York: Holt, Rinehart and Winston.

Hadden, Sally E. 2001. *Slave Patrols: Law and Violence in Virginia and the Carolinas*. Cambridge, MA: Harvard University Press.

Haley, Sarah. 2016. *No Mercy Here: Gender, Punishment, and the Making of Jim Crow Modernity*. Chapel Hill: University of North Carolina Press.

Hall, Stuart, Chas Critcher, Tony Jefferson, John Clarke, and Brian Roberts. 1978. *Policing the Crisis: Mugging, the State, and Law and Order*. London: Macmillan.

Hansford, Justin. 2016. "Community Policing Reconsidered: From Ferguson to Baltimore." In *Policing the Planet: Why the Policing Crisis Led to Black Lives Matter*, edited by Jordan T. Camp and Christina Heatherton, 215–25. London: Verso.

Hartman, Saidiya. 2019. *Wayward Lives, Beautiful Experiments: Intimate Histories of Social Upheaval*. New York: W. W. Norton.

Harvey, David. 2001. "Globalization and the 'Spatial Fix.'" *Geographische Revue: Zeitschrift für Literatur und Diskussion* 3 (2): 23–30.

Hedlund, Sarah. 2022. "George W. Meads: Rockville's One-Man Fire Department." YouTube, January 11. https://www.youtube.com/watch?v=39UxMDTNrro.

Hemphill, Katie M. 2020. *Bawdy City: Commercial Sex and Regulation in Baltimore, 1790–1915*. New York: Cambridge University Press.

Heynen, Nik, and Megan Ybarra. 2021. "On Abolition Ecologies and Making 'Freedom as a Place.'" *Antipode* 53 (1): 21–35. https://doi.org/10.1111/anti.12666.

Hill, Retha. 1991. "Md.'s Lincoln Park Community Celebrates a Century of Survival." *Washington Post*, June 30.

Hinton, Elizabeth. 2021. *America on Fire: The Untold History of Police Violence and Black Rebellion since the 1960s*. New York: Liveright.

Hobart, Mike. 2018. "Stagger Lee—from a Bar-Room Brawl to Black Resistance." *Financial Times*, July 11. https://ig.ft.com/life-of-a-song/stagger-lee.html.

Hodges, H. Eugene. 1971. "How to Lose the Hounds: Technology of the Gullah Coast Renegade." In *The Not So Solid South: Anthropological Studies in a Regional Subculture*, edited by J. Kenneth Morland, 66–73. Southern Anthropological Society Proceedings 4. Athens, GA: Southern Anthropological Society.

hooks, bell. 1989. "Choosing the Margin as a Space of Radical Openness." *Framework: The Journal of Cinema and Media* 36: 15–23.

Hosbey, Justin, and J. T. Roane. 2021. "A Totally Different Form of Living: On the Legacies of Displacement and Marronage as Black Ecologies." *Southern Cultures* 27 (1): 68–73. https://doi.org/10.1353/scu.2021.0009.

Housing Opportunities Commission of Montgomery County. 2018. "Comprehensive Annual Financial Report for the Fiscal Year Ended June 30, 2018." http://www.hocmc.org/images/files/Publications/FY2018_Financial_Statement.pdf.

Hughes, Alexandra, Victoria Gruber, and Claire Rossmark. 2016. "Public Safety and Policing Workgroup Report and Recommendations." January. http://mgaleg.maryland.gov/pubs/committee/2016-psp workgroup-report.pdf.

INCITE! 2003. "Community Accountability Working Document: Principles/Concerns/Strategies/Models." March 5. https://incite-national.org/community-accountability-working-document/.

Interrupting Criminalization. 2020. "The Demand Is Still #DefundPolice: Lessons from 2020." https://www.interruptingcriminalization.com/defundpolice-update.

Jacobs, Michelle S. 2017. "The Violent State: Black Women's Invisible Struggle against Police Violence." *William and Mary Journal of Race, Gender, and Social Justice* 24 (1): 39–100.

Jenkins, Morris. 2006. "Gullah Island Dispute Resolution: An Example of Afrocentric Restorative Justice." *Journal of Black Studies* 37 (2): 299–319. https://doi.org/10.1177/0021934705277497.

Jimenez, Maria. 2000. "The U.S-Mexico Border: A Strategy of Low-Intensity Conflict." *Social Justice* 27 (4): 32–36.

Joseph, Miranda. 2002. *Against the Romance of Community*. Minneapolis: University of Minnesota Press.

Joyce, Ryan. 2017. "'Bitch out of hell': The Queer Urban Marronage of Assotto Saint." *Women & Performance: A Journal of Feminist Theory* 27 (2): 176–93. https://doi.org/10.1080/0740770x.2017.1315230.

Justice Committee. 1973. *Report of the Justice Committee on [Redacted] Investigation*. Human Relations Commission 1957–1996, Record Group 15: Boards and Commissions, Series VI: Justice Committee, 1967–1976, Compliance

Complaints (restricted folder). Montgomery County Archives, Montgomery History, Gaithersburg, MD.

Kaba, Mariame, and John Duda. 2017. "Towards the Horizon of Abolition: A Conversation with Mariame Kaba." The Next System Project, November 9. https://thenextsystem.org/learn/stories/towards-horizon-abolition -conversation-mariame-kaba.

Kelley, Robin D. G. 2002. *Freedom Dreams: The Black Radical Imagination*. Boston: Beacon.

Kershnar, Sara, Staci Haines, Gillian Harkins, Alan Greig, Cindy Wiesner, Mich Levy, Palak Shah, Mimi Kim, and Jesse Carr. 2007. "Toward Transformative Justice: A Liberatory Approach to Child Sexual Abuse and Other Forms of Intimate and Community Violence." Generation Five, June. http://www.generationfive.org/wp-content/uploads/2013/07/G5_Toward _Transformative_Justice-Document.pdf.

Köbben, A. J. F. 1969. "Law at the Village Level: The Cottica Djuka of Surinam." In *Law in Culture and Society*, edited by Laura Nader, 117–40. Chicago: Aldine.

Krueger-Henney, Patricia, and Jessica Ruglis. 2020. "PAR is a Way of Life: Participatory Action Research as Core Re-Training for Fugitive Research Praxis." *Educational Philosophy and Theory* 52 (9): 961–72. https://doi.org/10 .1080/00131857.2020.1762569.

LaRoche, Cheryl Janifer. 2014. *Free Black Communities and the Underground Railroad: The Geography of Resistance*. Urbana: University of Illinois Press.

Lawson, Victoria. 2007. "Geographies of Care and Responsibility." Presidential Address. *Annals of the Association of American Geographers* 97 (1): 1–11. https:// doi.org/10.1111/j.1467-8306.2007.00520.x.

Leaming, Hugo Prosper. 1979. "Hidden Americans: Maroons of Virginia and the Carolinas." PhD diss., University of Illinois at Chicago.

Lebrón Ortiz, Pedro. 2019. "Maroon Logics as Flight from the Euromodern." *Transmodernity: Journal of Peripheral Cultural Production of the Luso-Hispanic World* 9 (2): 1–20. https://doi.org/10.5070/t492046321.

Leone, Mark P., Cheryl Janifer LaRoche, and Jennifer J. Babiarz. 2005. "The Archaeology of Black Americans in Recent Times." *Annual Review of Anthropology* 34:575–98. https://doi.org/10.1146/annurev.anthro.34.081804.120417.

Levine, Harvey A. 2000. "The Resurrection of 'Scotland.'" *Montgomery County Story* 43 (2): 125–35.

Library of Congress. 2017. Dred Scott v. Sandford: Primary Documents in American History. https://www.loc.gov/rr/program/bib/ourdocs/dredscott .html#American.

Lichtenstein, Alex. 1996. *Twice the Work of Free Labor: The Political Economy of Convict Labor in the New South*. New York: Verso.

Lincoln Park Civic Association. 2016. "Bylaws." http://www.lincolnparkcivicasso ciation.com/wp-content/uploads/2016/12/LPCA_Bylaws.pdf.

Lincoln Park Civic Association. n.d. "Meetings and Events." Lincoln Park Civic
    Association. Accessed March 15, 2019. http://www.lincolnparkcivicassociation
    .com/meetings-events/.
Lippman, Thomas W. 1967. "Toby Town to Get Pre-Fab Buildings." *Washington
    Post*, October 1.
Lopez, Christy E. 2020. "Defund the Police? Here's What That Really Means."
    Washington Post, June 7.
Lowe, Lisa. 2015. *The Intimacies of Four Continents*. Durham, NC: Duke University
    Press.
Loyd, Jenna M., and Anne Bonds. 2018. "Where Do Black Lives Matter? Race,
    Stigma, and Place in Milwaukee, Wisconsin." *Sociological Review* 66 (4):
    898–918. https://doi.org/10.1177/0038026118778175.
Lussana, Sergio. 2018. "Reassessing Brer Rabbit: Friendship, Altruism, and Com-
    munity in the Folklore of Enslaved African-Americans." *Slavery and Abolition*
    39 (1): 123–46. https://doi.org/10.1080/0144039x.2017.1323705.
Magruder, Joe. 1976. "Ken-Gar: Tiny Black Community Makes Progress, but
    Slowly." *Montgomery County (MD) Sentinel*, March 25. Communities files—
    Ken Gar. Jane C. Sween Research Library and Special Collections, Mont-
    gomery History, Rockville, MD.
Maher, Geo. 2021. *A World without Police: How Strong Communities Make Cops Obso-
    lete*. New York: Verso.
Malm, Andreas. 2018. "In Wildness Is the Liberation of the World: On Maroon
    Ecology and Partisan Nature." *Historical Materialism* 26 (3): 3–37. https://doi
    .org/10.1163/1569206x-26031610.
Marenin, Otwin. 1998. "From Ipa to Ilea: Change and Continuity in U.S. Inter-
    national Police-Training Programs." *Police Quarterly* 1 (4): 93–126. https://doi
    .org/10.1177/109861119800100405.
Marronage. n.d. "Marronage." Accessed June 10, 2020. https://marronage.dk/.
Maryland General Assembly. 2021. "Bond Bill Fact Sheet for Lincoln Park
    Community Center." 2021 Regular Session. https://mgaleg.maryland.gov
    /2021RS/bond_initiatives/Lincoln_Park_Community_Center.pdf.
Maryland Historical Trust. n.d. "Haiti/Martin's Lane Survey District—State
    Historic Sites Inventory Form." Communities files—Haiti. Jane C. Sween Re-
    search Library and Special Collections, Montgomery History, Rockville, MD.
Maryland Journal and Baltimore Advertiser. 1789. "Frank; a Runaway Negro
    Lad. Four Dollars Reward." June 16. Maryland State Archives. https://
    msa.maryland.gov/megafile/msa/speccol/sc5400/sc5496/runaway
    _advertisements/pdf/17890616mjba1.pdf.
McDaniel, George W. 1979a. *Black Historical Resources in Upper Western Montgomery
    County, Maryland*. n.p.: Sugarloaf Regional Trails.
McDaniel, George W. 1979b. "Jerusalem: Founded on Faith and 'Concern for One
    Another.'" *Washington Post*, February 22.

McDaniel, George W. 1979c. *Reflections of Black Heritage: An Architectural and Social History of Black Communities in Montgomery County, Maryland*. n.p.: Sugarloaf Regional Trails.

McGuckian, Eileen. 1989. "Haiti, an Historic Black Community." *Montgomery County Story* 32 (1): 47–58.

McKittrick, Katherine. 2006. *Demonic Grounds: Black Women and the Cartographies of Struggle*. Minneapolis: University of Minnesota Press.

McKittrick, Katherine. 2011. "On Plantations, Prisons, and a Black Sense of Place." *Social and Cultural Geography* 12 (8): 947–63. https://doi.org/10.1080 /14649365.2011.624280.

McKittrick, Katherine. 2013. "Plantation Futures." *Small Axe: A Caribbean Journal of Criticism* 17 (3): 1–15. https://doi.org/10.1215/07990537-2378892.

McKittrick, Katherine. 2021. *Dear Science and Other Stories*. Durham, NC: Duke University Press.

McLeod, Allegra M. 2015. "Prison Abolition and Grounded Justice." UCLA *Law Review* 62:1156–1239.

"Memorandum: Reported Unrest in the Scotland Community." 1975. Human Relations Commission 1957–1996, Record Group 15: Boards and Commissions, Series VI: Justice Committee, 1967–1976, Compliance Complaints (restricted folder). Montgomery County Archives, Montgomery History, Gaithersburg, MD.

Merchant, Carolyn. 2003. "Shades of Darkness: Race and Environmental History." *Environmental History* 8 (3): 380–94. https://doi.org/10.2307/3986200.

Merriam-Webster. n.d. S.v. "holding ground." Accessed February 28, 2022. https://www.merriam-webster.com/dictionary/holding%20ground.

Meyer, Eugene L. 2018. "'GREAT EXCITEMENT. Runaway Slaves': The Slave Uprising That Maryland Seems to Want to Forget." *Washington Post*, July 7.

Meyersburg, Munro P. 1978. "A History of Ken-Gar." Communities files—Ken-Gar. Kensington Historical Society, Kensington, MD.

Miller, Chris. 2017. "Historically Black Ken-Gar Community Celebrates 125th Anniversary." *Capital News Service*, September 28. https://cnsmaryland.org/2017/09 /28/historically-black-ken-gar-community-celebrates-125th-anniversary/.

Mingus, Mia. 2019. "Transformative Justice: A Brief Description." *Transform Harm* (blog), January 11. https://transformharm.org/transformative-justice -a-brief-description/.

Mitchell, Timothy. 1999. "Society, Economy, and the State Effect." In *State/Culture: State-Formation after the Cultural Turn*, edited by George Steinmetz, 76–97. Ithaca, NY: Cornell University Press.

Mitric, Joan McQueeney. 1999. "Preserving the Past in Modest Ken-Gar." *Washington Post*, January 30.

Montgomery County, Maryland, Department of Police. 1972. "Summary—Carolyn Twyman Incident." Human Relations Commission. Justice Committee:

Correspondence, Memos, Reports. Montgomery County Archives, Montgomery History, Gaithersburg, MD.

Montgomery County, Maryland, Department of Police. 1982. *1982 Annual Report*. Record Group 7: Public Safety. Montgomery County Archives, Montgomery History, Gaithersburg, MD.

Montgomery County, Maryland, Department of Police. 1989. *1988 Annual Report*. Record Group 7: Public Safety. Montgomery County Archives, Montgomery History, Gaithersburg, MD.

Montgomery County, Maryland, Department of Police. 1993. "Demonstration Projects in Community Policing." Record Group 7: Public Safety. Montgomery County Archives, Montgomery History, Gaithersburg, MD.

Montgomery County, Maryland, Department of Police. 1995. *FY 95 Annual Report*. Record Group 7: Public Safety. Montgomery County Archives, Montgomery History, Gaithersburg, MD.

"Montgomery County Commission on Human Relations Minutes: June 28, 1965." 1965. Communities files—Tobytown. Jane C. Sween Research Library and Special Collections, Montgomery History, Rockville, MD.

Montgomery (MD) Journal. 1845. "Yesterday Morning Early." July 9. African Americans file—Newspaper Items. Jane C. Sween Research Library and Special Collections, Montgomery History, Rockville, MD.

Moskos, Peter C. 2008. "Two Shades of Blue: Black and White in the Blue Brotherhood." *Law Enforcement Executive Forum* 8 (5): 57–86.

Movement for Black Lives (M4BL). 2020a. "End the War on Black Communities." https://m4bl.org/wp-content/uploads/2020/06/01-End-the-War-on-Black -Communities.pdf.

Movement for Black Lives (M4BL). 2020b. "End the War on Black People: Introduction." https://m4bl.org/wp-content/uploads/2020/06/00-Preamble.pdf.

Movement for Black Lives (M4BL). 2020c. "End the War on Black Youth." https:// m4bl.org/wp-content/uploads/2020/06/02-End-the-War-on-Black-Youth .pdf.

[Moynihan, Daniel Patrick.] 1965. *The Negro Family: The Case for National Action*. Publication of the US Department of Labor, Office of Policy Planning and Research. Washington, DC: US Government Printing Office.

Mulroy, Kevin. 2003. *Freedom on the Border: The Seminole Maroons in Florida, the Indian Territory, Coahuila, and Texas*. Lubbock: Texas Tech University Press.

Murch, Donna. 2015. "Crack in Los Angeles: Crisis, Militarization, and Black Response to the Late Twentieth-Century War on Drugs." *Journal of American History* 102 (1): 162–73. https://doi.org/10.1093/jahist/jav260.

Mustaffa, Jalil Bishop. 2017. "Mapping Violence, Naming Life: A History of Anti-Black Oppression in the Higher Education System." *International Journal of Qualitative Studies in Education* 30 (8): 711–27. https://doi.org/10.1080 /09518398.2017.1350299.

Narrative Arts. n.d. "Prison Ecology Project | Nation Inside." Accessed March 26, 2021. https://nationinside.org/campaign/prison-ecology-project/.

Nopper, Tamara K. 2020. "Abolition Is Not a Suburb." *The New Inquiry* (blog), July 16. https://thenewinquiry.com/abolition-is-not-a-suburb/.

Northup, Solomon. (1853) 1997. *Twelve Years a Slave: Narrative of Solomon Northup, a Citizen of New-York, Kidnapped in Washington City in 1841, and Rescued in 1853* (electronic edition). Documenting the American South. University of North Carolina–Chapel Hill. https://docsouth.unc.edu/fpn/northup/northup.html.

"Notes from Conversation with John Vlach." 1988. Black History—Haiti—General Information. Peerless Rockville Historic Preservation Ltd., Rockville, MD.

Nurmi, Joy. 1990. "Dealers and Users Help in Weekly Anti-Drug Vigil." *Gazette* (Maryland), May 23. Newspaper clipping from interview participant's personal collection, Rockville, MD.

Nurmi, Joy. 1991. "Lincoln Park Residents Celebrate a Proud Century." *Gazette* (Maryland), July 3. Communities files—Lincoln Park. Jane C. Sween Research Library and Special Collections, Montgomery History, Rockville, MD.

Ocasio-Cortez, Alexandria. 2019. "Recognizing the Duty of the Federal Government to Create a Green New Deal; H.Res. 109–116th Congress (2019–2020)." [US] Congress. https://www.congress.gov/bill/116th-congress/house-resolution/109.

Oide, Thomas, and Torey Van Oot. 2021. "Mapped: How the Minneapolis Police Charter Amendment Vote Failed." *Axios*, November 4. https://www.axios.com/local/twin-cities/2021/11/04/minneapolis-police-charter-amendment-vote-mapped.

Oparah, Julia Chinyere. 2015. "Maroon Abolitionists: Black Gender-Oppressed Activists in the Anti-Prison Movement in the US and Canada." In *Captive Genders: Trans Embodiment and the Prison Industrial Complex*, 2nd ed., edited by Eric A. Stanley and Nat Smith, 327–56. Oakland, CA: AK Press.

P.A.C. Spero & Company. 1997. "Woodlawn Manor—Maryland Historical Trust Historic Sites Inventory Form." M-28-14. https://mht.maryland.gov/secure/medusa/PDF/Montgomery/M;%2028-14.pdf.

Pathik, Carol. 1975. "County Blacks: They Came a Long Way." *Montgomery (MD) Journal*, April 17. African Americans file—Newspaper Items. Jane C. Sween Research Library and Special Collections, Montgomery History, Rockville, MD.

Phelps, Mary-Ellen. 1991. "Lincoln Park Celebrates Its 100th Anniversary." *Montgomery (MD) Journal*, February 11. Communities files—Lincoln Park. Jane C. Sween Research Library and Special Collections, Montgomery History, Rockville, MD.

Phibbs, Pat. 1990. "Scotland Residents Fight for Improvement." *Gazette* (Maryland), August 30. Communities files—Scotland. Jane C. Sween Research Library and Special Collections, Montgomery History, Rockville, MD.

Porter, Pamela. 1988. "Blacks Try to Preserve Their Land, Heritage." *Montgomery (MD) Journal*, November 15. African Americans file—Communities. Jane C. Sween Research Library and Special Collections, Montgomery History, Rockville, MD.

Port Tobacco Times, and Charles County Advertiser. 1845. "Untitled." November 6. Chronicling America: Historic American Newspapers, Library of Congress, Washington, DC. https://chroniclingamerica.loc.gov/lccn/sn89060060/1845-11-06/ed-1/seq-2/.

Port Tobacco Times, and Charles County Advertiser. 1846. "Broke Jail." March 26. Chronicling America: Historic American Newspapers, Library of Congress, Washington, DC. https://chroniclingamerica.loc.gov/lccn/sn89060060/1846-03-26/ed-1/seq-3/.

Port Tobacco Times, and Charles County Advertiser. 1850. "Untitled." November 27. Chronicling America: Historic American Newspapers, Library of Congress, Washington, DC. https://chroniclingamerica.loc.gov/lccn/sn89060060/1850-11-27/ed-1/seq-2/.

President's Task Force on Urban Renewal. 1970. "Urban Renewal: One Tool among Many; the Report of the President's Task Force on Urban Renewal." https://hdl.handle.net/2027/mdp.39015028082124.

Price, Richard, ed. 1973. *Maroon Societies: Rebel Slave Communities in the Americas*. Garden City, NY: Anchor.

Price, Richard. 1975. *Saramaka Social Structure: Analysis of a Maroon Society in Surinam*. Río Piedras: Institute of Caribbean Studies, University of Puerto Rico.

Price, Richard. 1976. *The Guiana Maroons: A Historical and Bibliographical Introduction*. Baltimore: Johns Hopkins University Press.

Price, Richard. 1996. *Maroon Societies: Rebel Slave Communities in the Americas*. 3rd ed. Baltimore: Johns Hopkins University Press.

Pulido, Laura, and Juan De Lara. 2018. "Reimagining 'Justice' in Environmental Justice: Radical Ecologies, Decolonial Thought, and the Black Radical Tradition." *Environment and Planning E: Nature and Space* 1 (1–2): 76–98. https://doi.org/10.1177/2514848618770363.

Quan, H. L. T. 2017. "'It's Hard to Stop Rebels That Time Travel': Democratic Living and the Radical Reimagining of Old Worlds." In *Futures of Black Radicalism*, edited by Gaye Theresa Johnson and Alex Lubin, 173–93. New York: Verso.

Rathner, Janet Lubman. 2005. "Generations of Residents Settle down in Scotland." *Washington Post*, June 18.

Reichel, Philip L. 1988. "Southern Slave Patrols as a Transitional Police Type." *American Journal of Police* 7 (2): 51–77.

Restorative Response Baltimore. n.d. "Restorative Practices." Accessed May 27, 2022. https://www.restorativeresponse.org/restorative-practices/.

Richardson, Valerie. 1988. "Lincoln Park Struggles to Retain Heritage in Face of Modern Woes." *Washington Times*, May 9.

Richie, Beth E. 2012. *Arrested Justice: Black Women, Violence, and America's Prison Nation*. New York: New York University Press.

Ritchie, Andrea J. 2017. *Invisible No More: Police Violence against Black Women and Women of Color*. Boston: Beacon.

Roane, J. T. 2018. "Plotting the Black Commons." *Souls* 20 (3): 239–66. https://doi .org/10.1080/10999949.2018.1532757.

Roberts, Andrea R. 2018. "Count the Outside Children! Kinkeeping as Preservation Practice among Descendants of Texas' Freedom Colonies." *Forum Journal* 32 (4): 64–74. https://doi.org/10.1353/fmj.2018.0022.

Roberts, Andrea R. 2020. "Haunting as Agency: A Critical Cultural Landscape Approach to Making Black Labor Visible in Sugar Land, Texas." *ACME: An International Journal for Critical Geographies* 19 (1): 210–44. https://acme-journal .org/index.php/acme/article/view/1752.

Roberts, Neil. 2015. *Freedom as Marronage*. Chicago: University of Chicago Press.

Robinson, Cedric J. (1983) 2000. *Black Marxism: The Making of the Black Radical Tradition*. Chapel Hill: University of North Carolina Press.

Rodrigues, Thiago. 2015. "Drug-Trafficking and Security in Contemporary Brazil." In *World Politics of Security*, edited by Felix Dane, 235–50. International Security: A European–South American Dialogue. Rio de Janeiro: Konrad-Adenauer-Stiftung.

Rodriguez, Akira Drake. 2021. *Diverging Space for Deviants: The Politics of Atlanta's Public Housing*. Athens: University of Georgia Press.

Rousey, Dennis C. 1996. *Policing the Southern City: New Orleans, 1805–1889*. Baton Rouge: Louisiana State University Press.

Rovner, Sandy. 1967. "Quiet Move to Integrate Montgomery Police May Pay Off." *The Sun* (Baltimore), November 26. Black History files—NAACP activities in Rockville. Peerless Rockville Historic Preservation Ltd., Rockville, MD.

Rozenfeld, Yelena, Jennifer Beam, Haley Maier, Whitney Haggerson, Karen Boudreau, Jamie Carlson, and Rhonda Medows. 2020. "A Model of Disparities: Risk Factors Associated with COVID-19 Infection." *International Journal for Equity in Health* 19 (1): 126. https://doi.org/10.1186/s12939-020 -01242-z.

Saleh, Amam Z., Paul S. Appelbaum, Xiaoyu Liu, T. Scott Stroup, and Melanie Wall. 2018. "Deaths of People with Mental Illness during Interactions with Law Enforcement." *International Journal of Law and Psychiatry* 58 (May–June): 110–16. https://doi.org/10.1016/j.ijlp.2018.03.003.

Samara, Tony Roshan. 2010. "Policing Development: Urban Renewal as Neo-Liberal Security Strategy." *Urban Studies* 47 (1): 197–214. https://doi.org/10 .1177/0042098009349772.

Sances, Michael W., and Hye Young You. 2017. "Who Pays for Government? Descriptive Representation and Exploitative Revenue Sources." *Journal of Politics* 79 (3): 1090–94. https://doi.org/10.1086/691354.

Sayers, Daniel O. 2014. *A Desolate Place for a Defiant People: The Archaeology of Maroons, Indigenous Americans, and Enslaved Laborers in the Great Dismal Swamp.* Gainesville: University Press of Florida.

"SCAT! Scotland Community Action Team." n.d. Black History files—Mont. Co. Areas. Peerless Rockville Historic Preservation Ltd., Rockville, MD.

Schept, Judah. 2015. *Progressive Punishment: Job Loss, Jail Growth, and the Neoliberal Logic of Carceral Expansion.* New York: New York University Press.

Schrader, Stuart. 2019. *Badges without Borders: How Global Counterinsurgency Transformed American Policing.* American Crossroads. Oakland: University of California Press.

Scott, James C. 1998. *Seeing like a State: How Certain Schemes to Improve the Human Condition Have Failed.* New Haven, CT: Yale University Press.

Scott, James C. 2009. *The Art of Not Being Governed: An Anarchist History of Upland Asia.* New Haven, CT: Yale University Press.

Scott, Julius S. 2020. *The Common Wind: Afro-American Currents in the Age of the Haitian Revolution.* New York: Verso.

Seigel, Micol. 2018. *Violence Work: State Power and the Limits of Police.* Durham, NC: Duke University Press.

Seigel, Micol. 2020. "Speaking of Police." *Society and Space*, October 1. https://www.societyandspace.org/articles/speaking-of-police.

Senate Bill 42. 2013. https://legiscan.com/MD/text/SB42/2013.

Shaffner, Tal. P. 1862. *The War in America: Being an Historical and Political Account of the Southern and Northern States: Showing the Origin and Cause of the Present Secession War. With a Large Map of the United States.* London: London Printing and Publishing Co.

Shakur, Assata. 1998. "An Open Letter from Assata Shakur." Texas ScholarWorks, University of Texas Libraries. http://hdl.handle.net/2152/6046.

Shapiro, Ari, Alex Vitale, and Derecka Purnell. 2020. "Defunding the Police: What Would It Mean for the U.S.?" NPR, June 11. https://www.npr.org/2020/06/11/875311086/defunding-the-police-what-would-it-mean-for-the-u-s.

Sharpe, Christina. 2016. *In the Wake: On Blackness and Being.* Durham, NC: Duke University Press.

Shaver, Katherine. 2016. "Tobytown Finally Gets a Bus." *Washington Post*, May 27.

Shoatz, Russell Maroon. 2013. *Maroon the Implacable: The Collected Writings of Russell Maroon Shoatz.* Edited by Fred Ho and Quincy Saul. Chicago: PM Press.

Shoemaker, Sandy M. 1994. "'We Shall Overcome, Someday': The Equal Rights Movement in Baltimore 1935–1942." *Maryland Historical Magazine* 89 (3): 261–74.

Siegel, Joyce B. 1973. Oral History of Joyce B. Siegel. Transcript. Montgomery County Archives, Montgomery History, Gaithersburg, MD.

Simone, AbdouMaliq. 2004. "People as Infrastructure: Intersecting Fragments in Johannesburg." *Public Culture* 16 (3): 407–29. https://doi.org/10.1215/08992363-16-3-407.

Simpson, Bob. 2013. "Turning around Racism." SocialistWorker.Org, November 21. https://socialistworker.org/2013/11/21/turning-around-racism.

Singh, Jai. 1981. "Tobytown: A Decade Later." *Montgomery (MD) Journal*, February 13. Communities files—Tobytown. Jane C. Sween Research Library and Special Collections, Montgomery History, Rockville, MD.

Smith, Neil. 1992. "Contours of a Spatialized Politics: Homeless Vehicles and the Production of Geographical Scale." *Social Text* 33:54–81. https://doi.org/10.2307/466434.

Soderberg, Susan. 1992. "Freed Slaves Founded County Communities after the Civil War." *Gazette* (Maryland), February 12, sec. Up-County Remembered. African Americans file—Communities. Jane C. Sween Research Library and Special Collections, Montgomery History, Rockville, MD.

Sojoyner, Damien M. 2016. *First Strike: Educational Enclosures in Black Los Angeles.* Minneapolis: University of Minnesota Press.

Spice, Anne. 2018. "Fighting Invasive Infrastructures: Indigenous Relations against Pipelines." *Environment and Society* 9 (1): 40–57. https://doi.org/10.3167/ares.2018.090104.

Stieff, Betsy. 1991. "Delving into Lincoln Park Past." *Rockville Express*, June 13. Communities files—Lincoln Park. Jane C. Sween Research Library and Special Collections, Montgomery History, Rockville, MD.

Still, William. 1872. *The Underground Rail Road. A Record of Facts, Authentic Narratives, Letters, &c., Narrating the Hardships, Hair-Breadth Escapes, and Death Struggles of the Slaves in Their Efforts for Freedom, as Related by Themselves and Others, or Witnessed by the Author; Together with Sketches of Some of the Largest Stockholders and Most Liberal Aiders and Advisers of the Road.* Philadelphia: Porter & Coates.

Story, Brett. 2019. *Prison Land: Mapping Carceral Power across Neoliberal America.* Minneapolis: University of Minnesota Press.

Story, Brett, and Seth J. Prins. 2019. "A Green New Deal for Decarceration." *Jacobin*, August 28. https://jacobinmag.com/2019/08/green-new-deal-decarceration-environment-prison-incarceration.

Stovall, David. 2018. "Are We Ready for 'School' Abolition? Thoughts and Practices of Radical Imaginary in Education." *Taboo: The Journal of Culture and Education* 17 (1): 51–61. https://doi.org/10.31390/taboo.17.1.06.

Sugarland Ethno-History Project. 2020. *I Have Started for Canaan: The Story of the African American Town of Sugarland.* Poolesville, MD: Sugarland Ethno-History Project.

Taylor, Keeanga-Yamahtta. 2016. *From #BlackLivesMatter to Black Liberation.* Chicago: Haymarket.

Thomas, Lynnell L. 2020. "Maroon Colonies and New Orleans Neutral Grounds: From a Protosuburban Past to a Postsuburban Future." *Urban Geography* 41 (1): 21–26. https://doi.org/10.1080/02723638.2019.1614370.

Thompson, Alvin O. 2006. *Flight to Freedom: African Runaways and Maroons in the Americas*. Kingston, Jamaica: University of the West Indies Press.

Till, Karen E. 2012. "Wounded Cities: Memory-Work and a Place-Based Ethics of Care." *Political Geography* 31 (1): 3–14. https://doi.org/10.1016/j.polgeo.2011.10.008.

Tribune. 1972. "Tobytown Groundbreaking at Last." February 18. Communities files—Tobytown. Jane C. Sween Research Library and Special Collections, Montgomery History, Rockville, MD.

Tronto, Joan. 1993. *Moral Boundaries: A Political Argument for an Ethic of Care*. New York: Routledge.

US Government. 1974. "24 CFR Subpart B—Turnkey III Program Description." Code of Federal Regulations. https://www.ecfr.gov/current/title-24/subtitle-B/chapter-IX/part-904/subpart-B.

Vasudevan, Pavithra. 2019. "An Intimate Inventory of Race and Waste." *Antipode* 53 (3): 770–90. https://doi.org/10.1111/anti.12501.

Vitale, Alex S. 2017. *The End of Policing*. New York: Verso.

Wagandt, Charles Lewis. 2004. *The Mighty Revolution: Negro Emancipation in Maryland, 1862–1864*. 2nd ed. Baltimore: Maryland Historical Society.

Wagner, Arlo. 1991. "Enclave No Longer Model of Poverty." *Washington Times*, June 11.

Walsh, Elsa L. 1982. "It Takes More Than a Facelift to Change Toby Town's Soul." *Washington Post*, July 7.

Washington Area Spark. 1971. "Spark!" October 5. https://washingtonspark.files.wordpress.com/2019/04/1971-10-05-spark-vol-1-no-1.pdf.

Washington Area Spark. 1972a. "5 Ken-Gar Residents Arrested for Murder after Racists Attack Their Community." September 6. https://washingtonspark.files.wordpress.com/2015/10/spark-1972-09-06-vol-2-no-1.pdf.

Washington Area Spark. 1972b. "Investigation Begins into Woman's Death during Police Chase." October 31. https://washingtonspark.files.wordpress.com/2015/10/spark-1972-10-31-vol-2-no-3.pdf.

Washington Area Spark. 1972c. "Ken-Gar Has Long History of Harassment by White Racists." October 4. https://washingtonspark.files.wordpress.com/2015/10/spark-1972-10-04-vol-2-no-2.pdf.

Washington Post. 1969. "Local Population Explosion." January 14.

Webb Hooper, Monica, Anna María Nápoles, and Eliseo J. Pérez-Stable. 2020. "COVID-19 and Racial/Ethnic Disparities." *JAMA* 323 (24): 2466–67. https://doi.org/10.1001/jama.2020.8598.

Weber, Max. 1994. "The Profession and Vocation of Politics." In *Weber: Political Writings*, edited by Peter Lassman and Ronald Speirs, 309–69. Cambridge: Cambridge University Press.

Welsh, Barney. 1961. "Our Negro Leaders." *Sentinel*, September 28, sec. Welsh Rare Bit. African Americans file—Newspaper Items. Jane C. Sween Research Library and Special Collections, Montgomery History, Rockville, MD.

Wiener, Elizabeth. 1977. "Tobytown: Massive Infusions of Money, and Liberal Good Will Have Failed to Correct Problems in This Small Enclave of Slave Descendents [sic]." *Sentinel*, November 10. Communities files—Tobytown. Jane C. Sween Research Library and Special Collections, Montgomery History, Rockville, MD.

Williams, Kristian. 2007. *Our Enemies in Blue: Police and Power in America*. Cambridge, MA: South End.

Williams, Miriam J. 2017. "Care-Full Justice in the City." *Antipode* 49 (3): 821–39. https://doi.org/10.1111/anti.12279.

Williams, Yohuru. 2015. "You're Nobody 'Till Somebody Kills You: Baltimore, Freddie Gray and the Problem of History." *Huffington Post*, April 29. https://www.huffingtonpost.com/yohuru-williams/youre-nobody-till-somebod_b_7167028.html.

Wilson, James Q., and George L. Kelling. 1982. "Broken Windows." *Atlantic Monthly* 249 (3): 29–38.

Wims, William G. 1972. "Presented to the Commissioners under New Business, Tuesday, 9/26/72 HRC Meeting." Human Relations Commission. Justice Committee: Correspondence, Memos, Reports. Montgomery County Archives, Montgomery History, Gaithersburg, MD.

Wims, William G. 1973. "Report to the HRC Justice Committee." Human Relations Commission. Justice Committee: Correspondence, Memos, Reports. Montgomery County Archives, Gaithersburg, MD.

Winston, Celeste. 2020. "The Everyday Black Life of Abolition." *Black Perspectives* (blog), August 5. https://www.aaihs.org/the-everyday-black-life-of-abolition/.

Winston, Celeste. 2021. "Maroon Geographies." *Annals of the American Association of Geographers* 111 (7): 2185–99. https://doi.org/10.1080/24694452.2021.1894087.

Wintersmith, Robert F. 1974. *Police and the Black Community*. Lexington, MA: D. C. Heath.

Woods, Clyde. 1998. *Development Arrested: The Blues and Plantation Power in the Mississippi Delta*. New York: Verso.

Woods, Clyde, Laura Pulido, Jordan T. Camp, Mathew Coleman, Sapana Doshi, and Nik Heynen. 2017. *Development Drowned and Reborn: The Blues and Bourbon Restorations in Post-Katrina New Orleans*. Athens: University of Georgia Press.

Wraga, Monica P. 2001a. "Potomac's Black Communities Celebrate History." *Gazette* (Maryland), January 31. African Americans file—Newspaper Items. Jane C. Sween Research Library and Special Collections, Montgomery History, Rockville, MD.

Wraga, Monica P. 2001b. "Tobytown Residents Look to Future." *Gazette* (Maryland), January 31. Communities files—Tobytown. Jane C. Sween Research Library and Special Collections, Montgomery History, Rockville, MD.

Wraga, Monica P. 2003. "Housing Commission, Tobytown Community Agree." *Gazette* (Maryland), January 8. Communities files—Tobytown. Jane C. Sween Research Library and Special Collections, Montgomery History, Rockville, MD.

Wright, Willie Jamaal. 2018. "As Above, So Below: Anti-Black Violence as Environmental Racism." *Antipode* 53 (3): 1–19. https://doi.org/10.1111/anti.12425.

Wright, Willie Jamaal. 2020. "The Morphology of Marronage." *Annals of the American Association of Geographers* 110 (4): 1–16. https://doi.org/10.1080/24694452.2019.1664890

Wynter, Sylvia. 1970. "Jonkonnu in Jamaica: Towards the Interpretation of Folk Dance as a Cultural Process." *Jamaica Journal* 4 (2): 34–48.

Zielinski, Alex. 2019. "Mayor Wheeler Considers Eugene's Model of Mental Health First." *Portland (OR) Mercury*, January 28. https://www.portlandmercury.com/news/2019/01/28/25620179/mayor-wheeler-considers-eugenes-model-of-mental-health-first-response.

Index

Black communities (continued)
subsistence strategies in, 93–97; urban renewal and targeting of, 54–62

Black flight: as agency, 36; atomization of, 14–16; folklore tradition around, 17, 22–29; history of marronage and, 37–40, 64; maroon geographies and, 1–3, 10–16, 30–36, 117–18; maroon troop escape attempt, 40–42; marronage and, 1; police violence and, xiii–xiv, xvi–xix; policing and, 17, 21–22, 64, 117–18; Twyman crisis and, 42–51; vocabulary of, 135n2

Black geographies scholarship, maroon geographies and, 1–4

Black Joy Sundays, 126

Black life-making, maroon geographies and, 122

Black Lives Matter, 8, 110, 126

Black Panther Party for Self-Defense, 33

Black Reconstruction in America (Du Bois), 114

Black refusal: fugitive infrastructure and, 39; Twyman case and, 45–51

Black Visions Collective, 126

Black women: education for, 77; marronage and, 83–84; police violence and positioning of, 50–51

Black Youth Project 100, 8, 110

Blair, Montgomery, 24

Blue Mash, Maryland, 26

blues epistemology, Black folklore and, 22–23

bodily surveillance, roots in slavery of, 6–7

Bonilla, Yarimar, 84–85

Bourdieu, Pierre, 135n3

Bratton, William, 123

Brazil, policing in, 123, 125–26

Brer Rabbit, in Black folklore, 27–28

Broadneck, Martin, 24, 30

Broadus, Thomas, xiii–xiv, xvi–xix, 91

broken windows policing, 78, 123–24

Browne, Simone, xiii, 136n4

Caesar, Mark, 41

CAHOOTS (Crisis Assistance Helping Out On The Streets), 118

Campaign Zero #8CantWait campaign, 113

Canada, fugitives from slavery in, 24–25

Canada Jim (James Wesley Hill), 24–25

Candler, Daniel Hayes, 41

carceral power: abolition policy and, 114–16; Black folklore and, 29; carceral habitus and, 135n3; communities and, 89–90; educational spaces and, 100; fugitive infrastructure and, 45, 52; maroon geographies and, 118–22; neoliberal anti-state state and, 102–4; police reform and, 113–14; shadow carceral state and, 63–64

care ethics: abolition of policing and, 119–22; Black community praxis and, 90–97, 104–8; Black freedom and, 50–51; community-based accountability systems and, 71–72

caves, as shelters for fugitives from slavery, 23

Chambers, James, 60

children, community-based accountability and, 70–71

Cimarrona Guard (La Guardia Cimarrona), 125

Cissel, Samuel, 11

Citizens' Committee for Justice, xiv–xv, 133n1

Clark, VèVè, 124

Colombia, abolition of policing in, 125

colonialism, fugitive infrastructure and, 61–62

communal pig butchering, 94–95

community: complex nature of, 87–88. See also Black communities

community-based accountability: abolition of policing and, 120–22; Black churches and, 31, 67–72, 77–78; maroon justice and, 66–72, 77–83, 110–11; police abolition and, 109–11; structural solutions to harm and, 76–78

tion of, 8–16; maroon justice alternatives to, 78–85; militarization of, 133n3; neoliberal anti-state state and, 102–4; policymaking and, 111–13; reformism and entrenchment of, xvii–xviii, 112–14; slavery and, 5–8, 41–42; Twyman crisis and, 42–51. *See also* abolition of policing
policymaking: abolition of policing and, 114–16; policing and, 111–13
political economy, racialized policing and, 6–8
politics of mobility, 82–83
The Potomac (Gutheim), 11
praise houses (Gullah Coast region), 67–68, 136n1
Presidential Commission on Law Enforcement and the Administration of Justice, 112
prison abolition movement, 126–28
prison population: labor economy and, 6; statistics on, 7
Promise Zone (HUD), 63–64
property ownership: abolition of policing and, 119; Black residents' skepticism of, 92–93
provision ground ideology, 92
Public Safety and Policing Workgroup (2015), xvii

Quaker Society of Friends, abolitionism and, 12, 21, 135n1
Quan, H. L. T., 15, 37, 49
Queen Nanny of the Windward Maroons of Jamaica, 84

racial capitalism: abolition of policing and, 119–22; Black poverty and, 60–62; Black property ownership and, 92–93; care practices and, 91; community formation as resistance to, 88–91, 96–97; neoliberal anti-state state and, 102–4; policing in service of, 7–8; urban renewal and, 54–55, 62
racial violence: Black communities as refuge from, 87–91; legislation for ending

of, xvi; maroon view of criminality and, 73–76; Twyman case and, 45–51
Ragin, Rufus, 60
real estate development: abolition of policing and, 119; disintegration of Black communities and, 35–36; policing and, 63–64
Reconstruction, policing during, 6
Reese, Gwen, 23, 68, 70
reformist reform: abolitionist policymaking and, 115–16; policing and, xvii–xviii, 112–14
restorative justice: community conferencing and, 89; maroon justice models and, 17–18, 65–66
Restorative Response Center, 89
Rhodes, Annie, 53
Roberts, Andrea R., 61
Roberts, Neil, 2
Robinson, Cedric J., 2
Roosevelt, Franklin D., 115

safety and security: Black communities' initiatives for, 87–91, 99–108; care environments and, 91–97; harm response teams, 76–78, 117–18
Sandy Spring, Maryland: abolitionism in, 21, 23–25, 135n1; Black property ownership in, 92–93; community-based accountability in, 67, 106–8; development in, 36; history of, 12–16, 34; newcomers in, 105–6; subsistence strategies in, 94–95
Scales, Howard, 77–78
Schept, Judah, 135n3
Scotland, Maryland, 12–16, 27; Black churches in, 95; Black community praxis in, 90–91; Black property ownership in, 93; community-based justice in, 79–80; maroon view of criminality in, 76; safety and security in, 105–6
Scotland Community Action Team (SCAT!), 80, 137n2
Scotland Community Office, 80
Scotland Mentoring Program, 80